Pocket Dictionary
of Ethnic Foods

Pocket Dictionary of Ethnic Foods

Definitions for common dishes and food terms from 42 ethnic groups, including:

Afghan	Latin American
Brazilian	Malaysian
Cajun/Creole	Mexican
Caribbean	Middle Eastern
Chinese	Moroccan
Cuban	Nepalese/Newar
Ethiopian	Persian
Filipino	Russian
French	Senegalese
German	South American
Greek	Southern/Soul Food
Indian/Pakistani	Spanish
Indonesian	Thai
Italian	Turkish
Jamaican	Vietnamese
Japanese	West African
Jewish	and many others
Korean	

Daniel G. Blum

Word Craft Publishing
WASHINGTON, DC

Although the author and publisher have made every effort to ensure the accuracy and completeness of information contained in this book, we assume no responsibility for errors, inaccuracies, omissions, or any inconsistency herein. Any slights of people, places, or organizations are unintentional.

Marmite® is a registered trademark of Bestfoods UK Ltd.
Milo® is a registered trademark of Nestle Group.
UGLI® is a registered trademark of Cabel Hall Citrus Limited.
Vegemite® is a registered trademark of Kraft Foods Ltd.

First printing 2005

ISBN 0-9754894-3-7
LCCN 2004106150

TABLE OF CONTENTS

ACKNOWLEDGMENTS

The author would like to express his thanks to the many friends who contributed to the assembling and production of this guide. Living in Washington, D.C. has placed him close to thousands of ethnic food establishments and experts. Since the nation's capital hosts the official diplomatic community and serves as a magnet for an extremely diverse immigrant community, it is the ideal environment for learning about and enjoying ethnic foods. The author specifically recognizes the contributions of the following persons whose generous help made this volume possible:

Mr. Balraj Bhasin of Bombay Curry Company in Alexandria, Virginia for very generously sharing his detailed knowledge of Indian foods (comprising the most numerous definitions of all the cuisines in this book); Liberata Ehemba of Chez Auntie Libe restaurant in Washington for her assistance with Senegalese and African definitions; Esmail Dehi of the Caravan Grill near Dupont Circle for sharing the wisdom earned in fifty years as a chef of Persian cuisine; Renford Powell of Euphoria restaurant and bar in the District for sharing his knowledge of Jamaican and Caribbean food; Tony Shallal of Skewers Restaurant near Dupont Circle for helping me to understand Middle Eastern foods and to translate certain Arabic terms; Rita Susetio at Satay Sarinah restaurant in Alexandria and Elly Benjamin of Ivy's Place in Washington for explaining the styles of cuisines in the islands of Indonesia; Ladavan Srigatesook and Supida Piwkhow of Dusit Thai restaurant in Silver Spring, Maryland for their clarification of Thai food terms and pronunciations; Hyun Soo Kim, the chef at Hee Been Restaurant in Alexandria for our dialog about Korean food names and ingredients; Alcy De Souza, owner of The Grill from Ipanema in Adams Morgan, for sharing his in-depth knowledge of Brazilian dishes; Mr. Y.F. Lee of the Hunan Herndon in Herndon, Virginia for his help in taking the mystery out of Chinese food terms; Hemanta Shrestha and Buddha Maharjan of Mt. Everest Restaurant in Washington for their assistance in distinguishing the foods and cultures of Nepal and Tibet; Mr. Hafiz Abbasi of the Afghan Restaurant in Alexandria for his assistance with Afghan foods; Tin T. Quan of Saigonnais restaurant in Adams Morgan for his in-depth explanation and samples of Vietnamese food definitions and pronunciation; Nailya Alexander of Washington for her detailed briefings about contemporary Russian cuisine and translation of traditional recipes; Alexandra Costra of Maxim Restaurant in Washington for her explanation of certain Russian restaurant dishes and related ethnic foods; Santi Zabaleta of Taberna del Alabardero in Washington for his help in understanding Spanish cuisine terms; Elizabeth Bright of Coppi's Restaurant in Washington for an education on Italian food terms; Lex Saeng-plai of Lex Cajun Grill in Washington for his discussion of Cajun dishes; Florence Devilliers, owner of Lavandou Restaurant in Cleveland Park for her help with French cooking terms; my friend Glenn Germaine for sharing his knowledge of Mexican, Central American, and South American foods; my friends Doris Kuehn and Ellen Blankhertz for their extensive help in fact-checking German food definitions; Rick Zemlin for sharing his knowledge of foods of the Philippine Islands; Mr. Emmanuel Bobga of Roger Miller Restaurant in Silver Spring for his assistance with Cameroonian and West African foods; Atsuko Shigihara of Art at the Confluence of East and West for her help with Japanese definitions; John Eshun of Vicino restaurant for sharing his knowledge of Italian foods; Cavit Ozturk of Café Divan in Washington for his help in understanding a wide variety of Turkish foods; Abdelhak Abdelmoumen, owner of Taste of Morocco in Arlington Virginia, for his great demonstration and explanation of Moroccan foods; Getahun Admasu of the Ethio Store in Silver Spring for his extensive guidance in Ethiopian food definitions; my anonymous Venezuelan-American client for telling me all about arepas; Cheryl Stepanek for sharing her cultural heritage and knowledge of Ukrainian and Polish food items; Maria Serrano, owner of Andalucia Spanish Restaurant in Rockville, Maryland for her clarification of some menu items; Pete Gouskos, owner of the Parthenon Restaurant in Washington, for our discussion of Greek dishes; Stacey King for assisting me in putting together the Malaysian definitions; Piero Ricchiari of Il Pizzico Ristorante in Rockville, Maryland for confirming some Italian food definitions; Rev. Justiniano Cruz for his help with Colombian dishes; Kirsten Burgard of Washington for her clarification of West African cooking terms; and John Kurtz of Southside 815 Restaurant in Alexandria for his helpful discussion of Cajun and Southern food terms. Thanks also to Justice, owner of Bukom Café in Washington, for his help with Ghanaian and West African dishes; Assefa Woldesenbet of Nile Market in Washington for his explanation of certain Ethiopian terms; Gerri Thompson of Oxon Hill, Maryland who shared her expertise in Southern and Soul food cooking; Harriett Dorn of Arlington for her assistance with traditional Jewish dishes; Hervé Sorel for his guidance on contemporary French dining; Mike Zand of the Village Green Grill House of Kebob in Gaithersburg, MD for fact-checking the Persian definitions; Cindy Roberts of the Food Safety Education Information Center for her advice regarding food safety notes; and Dr. Mark Kantor of the University of Maryland Department of Nutrition and Food Science for his comments on food safety. I would also like to acknowledge Leah Sungenis for her suggestions regarding the introduction and for advice about Latvian and Italian foods; Robin Morse Mayers for her encouragement and for identifying publishing consultants; Philippe Blum of Group 5 Graphics for his guidance on page preparation and printing matters; Carol Herndon, Esq., for her suggestions regarding copyright and other legal matters. Thanks also to editor Allan Burns, Dick Hanna for the cover design, Cathy Bowman for typesetting, Debi Flora who was instrumental in coordinating the printing and production process, and to Deb Ellis, Jennifer Quintana and Kate Deubert for their unique professional assistance. A special thank you to Jacqueline Richman for putting up with me being glued to the computer for so long.

PREFACE

In the past few decades, the world of food in North America has been infused with a new vitality. American foods have always been marked by some variety, owing to the distinct ethnic origins of its native, European, African, Hispanic, and Asian ancestors. But the recent (and sometimes sudden) arrival of people born in other parts of the world has brought a proliferation of "new" ethnic foods to the major urban areas where such newcomers have settled. Thanks to the people of many cultures who have made this country their home, America is now host to the most wildly diverse kitchen in the world.

For many of us, there was little in our upbringing that prepared us to take advantage of the enormous variety of cuisines and dishes available to us. Presumably well-rounded people of otherwise bold disposition may, like the author, feel that they are in foreign territory when first encountering such foods. Who hasn't had the experience of sitting down in a new, unfamiliar restaurant and of being presented with a menu that is in a foreign language or mostly unintelligible? You may have hesitated to try to pronounce the name of some exotic item, let alone to put it in your mouth! You wondered, is it served hot or cold? Spicy or bland? Do you eat it with your hands, or a fork, or chopsticks? And most importantly, are there any frog's brains or other bizarre stuff in there? The staff is often helpful, sometimes not, in addressing these concerns. After a while, many of us who visit ethnic restaurants have settled on one or two "safe" dishes, which we order repeatedly, and we don't look at what else might be available. But when we don't, we are missing out on the rest of the incredible universe of sensation. No one (except perhaps the professional restaurant critics and their full-time students) will be familiar with *all* types of cuisines. This dictionary was created for ethnic food novices who would like to enter (literally) a whole new world of eating, as well as ethnic food aficionados who would like to extend their knowledge and pleasure.

It is the author's intention that this book be used as a guide by restaurant patrons while placing orders at their local establishments and by shoppers while visiting ethnic grocery stores. Ethnic cuisines often differ in America from foods in their country of origin, as chefs adapt to locally-available ingredients and customer expectations. Although some effort has been made here to distinguish the authentic character of dishes, the descriptions and emphasis mostly reflect American versions. With this caveat, travelers may find this guide useful as well.

At the outset of this project the author was far from being an "expert" on ethnic foods. To the contrary, assembling this dictionary was an attempt to quell his own ignorance and to compile his findings for others. The first thing one confronts in this research is the overwhelming variety of food items, and the methods of preparation, regional styles, and languages used to describe them. In the dizzying realm of international foods, a guide such as this one will only cover the more common items and terms in each country's cuisine.

There is an emphasis here on tropical, sub-tropical, and East Asian cuisines, since those are the ones encountered most frequently by the author and that, previously, stumped him most often. Due to practical limitations of research, some countries' foods were not included or were not covered as extensively or thoroughly, and no disrespect is intended. If the reader would like to suggest any improvements, additions, or corrections, the author would be most grateful and would consider them carefully when preparing future editions. See the feedback page in the back of the book.

When using this book, bear in mind that the definitions are approximate and that you will find a huge variety of stylistic and regional variations among foods using the same name. Be prepared for a few surprises along the way. Have a drink, and collect your sense of humor.

This is not a cookbook. It is a pocket dictionary, to explain what an ethnic food is and how to pronounce it. For those desiring recipes or an understanding of the history, geography, and culture of ethnic foods, see some of the works mentioned in the bibliography, including links to websites offering an exhaustive treatment of these subjects.

I hope this will be as useful a guide for you as it has been for me. *Kali Orexi!**

12 May 2004

*Greek for *Bon Appetit*

IMPORTANT INFORMATION REGARDING THE SAFETY OF FOODS DESCRIBED IN THIS BOOK (DISCLAIMER)

When ordering foods at ethnic restaurants, purchasing items for sale in stores, or attending parties, do not rely on the definitions and descriptions contained in this book to make decisions regarding food safety. Since definitions in this book are approximate, they do not cover all the variations in ingredients and methods of preparation that you will encounter. You may find that a particular variation of the food you are eating contains ingredients not mentioned in this book or on a menu, which may cause an adverse or allergic reaction (peanuts, for example) or which may be potentially harmful. Therefore, always check with your restaurant manager, server, proprietor, or host to confirm descriptions of unfamiliar foods and to be safe regarding the presence or absence of any potentially harmful ingredients.

According to government food safety experts, pregnant women, young children, older adults, and those with compromised immune systems must be especially careful to avoid consuming partially cooked or raw meat, raw (uncooked or unpasteurized) eggs, raw seafood, unpasteurized milk, uncooked (soft) cheeses, and other animal products which are not fully cooked. (Uncooked soft cheeses include brie, Camembert, feta, queso blanco, queso fresco, asadero, Panela and Roquefort unless they are labeled as made with pasteurized milk.) According to the U.S. Food and Drug Administration, you are at increased risk if you suffer from liver disease or alcoholism, if you have decreased stomach acidity due to gastric surgery or the use of antacids, or if you have a compromised immune system due to steroid use, conditions such as AIDS, cancer, or diabetes, or treatments such as chemotherapy. If you or someone you are responsible for is in any of these categories, use extra caution when making ethnic food selections. When ordering, ask how an item is prepared and whether it is fully cooked. Federal food safety experts advise that persons in these at-risk populations also avoid eating all luncheon meats and deli meats, such as ham, and sliced prepared sausage meats, such as salami and mortadella, unless they are heated to a steaming hot temperature before they are served. Also, remember that it is always essential to refrigerate "doggie bags" and other take-out foods promptly. This advice and more is available at the Gateway to Federal Food Safety Information website at www.foodsafety.gov or other sites listed in the bibliography.

The Food Allergy & Anaphylaxis Network (FAAN) advises persons who are allergic to peanuts that African, Chinese, Indonesian, Mexican, Thai, and Vietnamese dishes often contain peanuts or are contaminated with peanuts during preparation of these types of meals. It is recommended that peanut-allergic individuals avoid these types of foods and restaurants. See www.foodallergy.org for further information.

Although a conscientious effort has been made to ensure the accuracy of the information in this book, it is not guaranteed. The author, publisher, and distributors of this book assume no responsibility for consequences resulting from the use of the information provided here.

GUIDE TO PRONUNCIATION

For many of the words listed in this volume, guides to pronunciation are offered, demarcated by forward slashes (/ ... /). These are not the formal guides to pronunciation one would find in a regular dictionary. Rather, they are ad-hoc approximations of the sounds that you might need to utter to be understood by a person with whom you are placing an order. Many of the pronunciations are written in "Anguish Languish" (English Language sounds produced by substituting similar-sounding words), a method of writing attributed to Howard L. Chace. For example, a classic Anguish Languish statement such as "Way dearth air safe lion mice hoop" approximates "Waiter, there's a fly in my soup." So it's not exact, but it's close enough for practical use.

You will find many sounds in other languages that have no equivalent in English and can only be approximated. Many consonants vary in their intensity and aspiration in ways that native English speakers might not easily perceive. The many vowel sounds uttered are quite different from the ones we are used to. And the variations in tone in some Asian languages cannot be readily discerned by the uninitiated nor printed using common English symbols. The pronunciations proposed in this book are the author's best attempt to be helpful within these limitations.

Constructions such as "hgh" and "hkh" represent the guttural sound widely used in German, Middle Eastern, and other languages. Syllables starting with "g" or "gh" represent the hard "g" sound as in "good," since the soft "g" is represented by the letter "j."

Pronunciation guides were omitted from words where the pronunciation could be intuitively derived from the spelling, as in the case of many of the Japanese words. When in doubt, do your best to guess, and remember *it's not the end of the world if you don't get it right.*

A

aamchur *see* **amchur**

aash, ash /rhymes with mosh/ [Persian] soup.

aash-e reshteh /ah-she-resh-tay/ [Persian] noodle soup.

abgousht, ab gousht /obb-goosht/ [Persian ("water meat")] a popular stew made with lamb shank or other meat, beans, and vegetables, all mashed together and typically served alongside the broth it was cooked in, with Iranian bread or rice and garnishes.

abish /ah-beesh'/ [Ethiopian] fenugreek seed, either whole or ground. *see also* **minchet abish**

acar /ah-char'/ [Indonesian] vegetables or fruits preserved with vinegar, for example pickles. *see also* **atjar, achar**

achar /ah-char'/ [Indian, other] traditional tangy, spicy pickled raw fruit or vegetable, such as lemon, mango, or tomato, preserved in oil.

achiote /ah-chee-oh'-tay/ [Latin American, other] the seeds or paste of a spice that imparts a yellow-orange color to foods. *also* **annatto**

ackee /ack'-ee/ [Jamaican (from West African *akye*)] a soft, bland, yellowish fruit resembling scrambled eggs when prepared, served hot, most commonly with salt fish.
(Note: ackee, which grows in pods, can be poisonous when unripe and must be left in the sun to mature until the pods open.)

Adana kebab /ah'-dah-nah-kuh-bob/ [Turkish, named after a town] spicy, grilled skewered meatballs.

adobo /uh-doe′-bo/ **1.** [Puerto Rican, Mexican, Filipino] a method of simmering (usually chicken or pork) in a marinade sauce of vinegar, garlic, and pepper with chiles or soy sauce. **2.** [Spanish] popular, traditional recipe for food items cured in vinegar, battered and fried.

adzuki, aduki *see* **azuki**

affumicato [Italian] smoked. *also* **affumicata**

agnello /on-yellow/ [Italian] lamb.

agnolotti /on-yo-lot′-tee/ [Italian] small half-moon-shaped pasta dumplings with a meat or cheese filling, similar to ravioli.

ahi /ah′-hee/ [Japanese] yellowfin tuna used for sushi.

aioli /I-owe-lee/ [French] a special strong-flavored mayonnaise sauce made with lots of garlic, olive oil, and egg yolk, originally from the region of Provence.
(*Note: foods prepared with raw [i.e., uncooked or unpasteurized] eggs may be unsafe for pregnant women, young children, older adults, and those with compromised immune systems.*)

airan *see* **ayran**

ais kacang *see* **ice kacang**

ajam *see* **ayam**

aji /ah′-hee/ [Peruvian, other] **1.** various kinds of South American hot chile peppers. **2.** a variable sauce made with aji chiles, oil, and other ingredients.

ajillo /ah′-hee-lo/ [Latin American] garlic sauce.

ajo /ah′-ho/ [Spanish, other] garlic.

ajo blanco [Spanish] a chilled creamy white soup made with almonds, garlic, and bread, garnished with grapes.

akara, akra /ock'-uh-rah/ [West African] fried bean cake, a flavorful appetizer or snack food made from ground black-eyed peas (with the skins removed) served with hot sauce and sometimes shrimp or fish. *also called* **kose**

akasa /ah-kah'-sah/ [West African] fermented corn dough porridge with milk eaten for breakfast.

a la brasa /ah-lah-brah'-sah/ [Latin American] cooked on an open charcoal grill.

a la parilla /ah-lah-pah-ree'-yah/ [various] on the grill.

albondigas /ahl-bohn'-dee-gus/ [Mexican] generic term for small meatballs made with various meats or fish, seasoned with chile peppers, herbs and spices, typically served in a flavorful soup or with a richly seasoned sauce.

al carbon /ahl-car-bohn'/ [Mexican] indicates an item grilled or cooked over charcoal or a wood fire.

al dente /al-don'-tay/ [Italian] a style of cooking pasta for fewer minutes so that it is firm and chewy rather than soft.

alecha /ah-letch'-uh/ [Ethiopian] a stew made with various vegetables (or meat) and mild seasonings such as turmeric and white pepper. *also* **allecha, alicha, alitcha, aleecha.**

Alfredo /all-fray'-doe/ [Italian-derived, originated in the U.S.] a rich, white pasta sauce made with butter, cream, and Parmesan cheese, originally prepared with raw egg and nutmeg.
(*Note: foods prepared with raw [i.e., uncooked or unpasteurized] eggs may be unsafe for pregnant women, young children, older adults, and those with compromised immune systems.*)

aloco *also* **alloco, aloko** [Cote d'Ivoire] sliced ripe plantains cooked in palm oil, either with sugar added or topped with a kind of salsa, sometimes with grilled fish or boiled eggs.

aloo, alu /ah-lew/ [Indian] potatoes.

aloo chaat /ah-lew-tchott/ [Indian] a snack consisting of deep-fried diced potatoes prepared with chaat seasoning. *see* **chaat masala**

aloo chole /ah-lew-cho'-lay/ [Indian] curried potatoes with chick peas.

aloo gobi [Indian] potatoes with cauliflower, typically with tomatoes and spices.

aloo ko achar /ah-lew-ko-ah-char/ [Nepalese] potato salad or potato chutney.

aloo matar /ah-lew-muh-tar/ [Indian] curried potatoes with green peas, cooked in a sauce.

aloo papri chat *see* **papri chat**

aloo paratha /ah-lew-pah-rah-tah/ [Indian] lightly fried soft whole-wheat flatbread filled with a potato and herb mixture, splashed with butter.

aloo saag /ah-lew-sahg/ [Indian] curried potatoes with greens (usually spinach).

aloo tama bodi [Nepalese] potatoes, bamboo shoots, and black-eyed peas cooked together, described as the national dish of Nepal.

al pastor *see* **tacos al pastor**

alu *see* **aloo**

amaranth /am'-uh-ranth'/ [South American, other] a leafy vegetable similar to spinach, bearing a high-protein seed.

amazu shoga [Japanese] pickled ginger, sliced thin. *see also* **gari**

ambasha /ahm-bah'-shah/ [Ethiopian] a decorated round raised bread with a spiced oil topping.

amchur [Indian] dried raw mango powder used as a spicy, very tangy flavoring agent. *also* **amchoor, aamchur**

Anaheim chile [Mexican] a long, narrow chile pepper with sweet taste, mild to moderately hot.

anchiote *see* **achiote**

ancho chile /ahn'-cho/ [Mexican] dried poblano chile with a sweet taste, mild to moderately hot.

andouille /on-dewey *or* ann-dewey/ **1.** [Cajun] a spicy smoked sausage with a robust flavor, made from pork, bacon, pork fat, garlic, spices, and salt, typically added to cooked dishes. **2.** [French, other] spiced organ meat sausage made with pork intestine, herbs, onion, and garlic, typically sliced thin and served cold as an appetizer.

andouillette /on-dwee-yet/ [French] small French andouille made with tripe, typically served hot as a main course item.

angel hair pasta [Italian] very thin stranded pasta. *see also* **cappellini**

annatto, annato *see* **achiote**

antipasto *plural* **antipasti** [Italian ("before the meal")] an appetizer served before the main meal.

antojitos /ahn-toe-hee'-toce/ [Mexican, other ("little whims")] **1.** appetizers. **2.** generic term for various popular food items or snacks (usually corn or tortilla-based) such as tacos, burritos, enchiladas, and tamales. **3.** [Salvadorean] a generic term for dishes designated as special "treats."

apple strudel [German/Austrian] finely sliced apples rolled and baked in multi-layered pastry dough, traditionally served with whipped cream. *also* **Apfelstrudel** /up'-fel-shtroo-dl/

arepa /ah-reh'-pah/ [Venezuelan, other] a round, bun-shaped corn-cheese patty or cake cooked in a hinged mold (called a *budare*) or fried, sometimes served with black beans or slit width-wise like a sandwich roll. Arepas are typically about four inches in diameter (except wider and thinner in Andes) and are made from a special variety of starchy, large-kernel corn.

arroz /ah-russ'/ [Spanish] rice.

arroz con leche /ah-russ'-con-ley'-cheh/ [Latin American] rice pudding dessert.

arroz con pollo /ah-russ'-con-poy'-oh/ [Latin American, Spanish] shredded chicken or chicken pieces cooked with rice, flavored with onion, garlic, bell pepper, olive oil, and various seasonings.

arroz dulce /ah-russ'-dool'-seh/ [Mexican ("sweet rice")] rice pudding flavored with cinnamon. *similar to* **arroz con leche**

arugula /ah-roo'-guh-luh/ [Italian] a popular, slightly bitter leafy salad green.

asada *see* **carne asada**

asadero [Mexican] a type of uncooked soft white cheese.
(*Note: government food safety experts advise pregnant women, older adults, and those with compromised immune systems not to eat asadero unless it is labeled as made with pasteurized milk or is thoroughly cooked to a boiling (bubbling) hot temperature.*

asado /ah-sah-doe/ [Argentine, other] roasted

beef, commonly cooked as the main focus of a major barbecue event.

asafoetida /ass-ah-fet′-id-ah/ [India, other ("stinking gum")] a strong-smelling spice, also called *hing*, containing a resin similar to garlic and onions, used in South Indian and Central Asian cooking. *also* **asafetida**

asam /ah-sahm/ [Indonesian, Malaysian] **1.** *n.* tamarind. **2.** a dish, such as vegetable, seafood, or pork, prepared with a spicy tamarind sauce. **3.** *adj.* sour.

asam manis [Indonesian] sweet and sour.

ash /rhymes with mosh/ [Persian] soup. *also* **aash**

asiago /ah-see-ah′-go/ [Italian] a firm, flavorful, light-colored cheese.

assa, asa /ah-sah/ [Ethiopian] fish.

atakilt, atikilt /ah-tah-kilt/ [Ethiopian] mixed vegetables.

atakilt wat /ah-tah-kilt-wutt/ [Ethiopian] a fresh vegetable stew, typically made with potatoes, cabbage, onions, carrots, or green beans, cooked with berbere (hot pepper seasoning).

atar /ah′-tar/ [Ethiopian] yellow or green split peas. *also* **ater**

atar allecha /ah′-tar-ah-letch′-uh/ [Ethiopian] mildly spiced pureed green or yellow split pea stew, served hot with injera.

ater *see* **atar**

atiéké, attieke /ah-chay′-keh/ [Cote d'Ivoire] boiled or steamed cassava flour or couscous.

atjar *more correctly* **acar** /ah-char/ [Indonesian] sweet-and-sour relish or pickles.

atole /ah-toh′-lay/ [Mexican] authentic porridge-like corn-flour beverage, sweetened and flavored with cinnamon, fruit, or chocolate, consumed hot with tamales.

aubergine /oh-bare-jheen/ [various] eggplant.

au gratin /oh-grah-taehn *or anglicized* oh-grot′-ten/ [French] prepared with grated Swiss cheese and cream or butter, which is melted on top and broiled to a crisp.

au jus /oh-jhoo/ [French] cooked in its own juices.

aush /owsh/ [Afghan] noodle and vegetable soup, typically including chopped spinach or lentils and a spoonful of yogurt.

aushak /ow-shack/ [Afghan] appetizer or entree consisting of ravioli-like dumplings filled with chopped scallions, topped with yogurt sauce and sometimes meat.

authentic [various] prepared in a manner closely resembling foods in the country of origin, using similar recipes and cooking methods, sometimes with imported ingredients.

avgolemono /ahv-ho-lay-mo′-no/ [Greek] a sauce made with lemon juice and raw eggs, which are partially cooked by contact when poured onto hot food items. Often served with dolmades (stuffed grape leaves).
(*Note: foods prepared with raw [i.e., uncooked or unpasteurized] eggs may be unsafe for pregnant women, young children, older adults, and those with compromised immune systems.*)

avgolemono soup /ahv-ho-lay-mo′-no/ [Greek] chicken-rice soup with cooked egg and lemon.

awaze /a-wah′-zeh/ [Ethiopian] a regionally variable spice mixture emphasizing hot chile peppers, sometimes with garlic and onion, typically prepared as a moist paste or sauce, or reconstituted from a dry awaze powder (equivalent to berbere) by adding a liquid such as wine or oil.

ayam *formerly* **ajam** /ah-yahm/ [Indonesian, Malaysian] chicken.

ayam asam manis [Indonesian] chicken prepared with sweet-and-sour sauce.

ayam opor *see* **opor ayam**

ayib /ah-eeb/ [Ethiopian] *see* **iab**

ayran [Turkish] popular unsweetened yogurt drink with a milk-like consistency. *also* **airan**

azidesse /ah-zuh-day′-say/ [West African] peanut stew with chicken, from Togo.

azuki /ah-zoo-kee/ [Japanese] dark red nutty beans. *also* **adzuki, aduki**

B

ba *see* **bahmi**

baati *see* **bati**

baba ghanoush, babaganouj /bah-bah-gah-noosh′/ [Lebanese, other ("spoiled old daddy")] roasted eggplant dip, made with garlic, sesame paste, and seasonings. Commonly served with pita bread.

babi /bobby/ [Indonesian] pork.

babotie *see* **bobotie**

bacalao, bacalhau /bock-allow/ [Portugese, other] salted dried cod, which is partially desalted by soaking in water, then cooked. Used in numerous recipes worldwide.

badam /bah-dahm *or* bah′-dum/ [Indian] almond.

bademjun /bah-dem-john′/ [Persian] eggplant.

badenjan /bah-den-john/ [Afghan] the word for tomato, but more often implying "black" badenjan, which is eggplant.

badenjan challaw /bah-den-john-chah-law/ [Afghan] chunks of meat simmered with eggplant, tomato, onion, garlic, and herbs, served with basmati rice.

badji /bah-jee/ [Jamaican] sautéed greens or other vegetables. *similar to* **bhaji**

bagna cauda /bah'-nyah-cow'-dah/ [Italian ("hot bath")] a creamy heated dip made with garlic and anchovies, usually served as an appetizer or party food, with vegetables for dipping on the side.

bagoong /bah-goh'-ong/ [Filipino] strong-smelling, salted, fermented shrimp or fish paste (or sauce) with an opaque purplish color, used in cooking.

baguette /bah-get/ [French] popular bread in the form of a long, skinny loaf with a well-defined crust, made with (strictly) flour, water, yeast, and salt.

Bahia, Baiana [Brazilian] a vernacular "soul food" style of cooking from the region of Bahia in northeastern Brazil, originally developed by African slaves, with a combination of African, Portuguese, and native influences, and often using dendé (palm oil) and coconut milk.

bahn *see* **banh**

bahmi /bah-mee'/ [Indonesian, Thai] egg noodle made with wheat flour. *also* **bakmi, ba mee, ba mi, bahmie**

bahmi goreng /go-rheng'/ [Indonesian] fried bahmi (noodles) mixed with shrimp and various meats and vegetables. *also* **bakmi goreng**

Baiana *see* **Bahia**

baingan /beng'-on/ [Indian ("without virtues")] eggplant. *also* **bhaigan, baigan, bengan, begon**

baingan bharta [Indian] mashed roasted eggplant, typically with tomatoes, onions, garlic, ginger, and spices.

Bajan [Caribbean] of or related to Barbados. Barbadian.

Bajan chicken [Caribbean] boneless chicken, which is stuffed with a very hot chile and herb mixture and baked, or breaded and fried, from Barbados.

bakes [Jamaican] a slightly sweet fried flatbread.

baklava, baklawa /bock-lah-vah'/ [Turkish, Greek, Middle Eastern] popular dessert pastry with alternating layers of filo dough and sugared chopped pistachios or walnuts, topped with syrup (sometimes honey).

bakmi *also* **bahmi** /bah-mee/ [Indonesian] egg noodles. *see also* **bahmi goring**

bakmi goreng / bah-mee go-rheng'/ [Indonesian] fried bakmi (noodles) mixed with shrimp and various meats and vegetables. *also* **bahmi goreng**

balachan, balacan /bah-lah-chan/ [Malaysian] *see* **shrimp paste**

baliadas /bah-lyah-dahss'/ [Honduran] popular snack consisting of a large, thick tortilla folded around some beans, lettuce, cilantro, and cream sauce.

balti [Indian ("bucket")] British term for a method of cooking originating in northwest India and Pakistan, based on dishes prepared and served in a karahi (wok-shaped metal pan), now widely popularized in the U.K and altered to include non-traditional recipes and ingredients. Such dishes may include a tangy curry mixture, coriander, onions, garlic, and green pepper. Typically accompanied by bread.

ba mi, ba mee [Thai] *see* **bahmi**

bamieh [Egyptian, other] okra and meat stew. *also* **bamia, bamya,** [Lebanese] **bamiyah**

bammy [Jamaican] fried flatbread made of cassava dough, usually soaked in milk and dipped in hot oil.

banchan /bahn-chahn/ [Korean] any small side dish. A collection of banchan are typically brought to the table with a meal in a Korean restaurant. *also* **ban chan**

bandeja /bahn-day′-ha/ [various] platter.

bandeja Paisa /bahn-day′-ha-pie′-sah/ [Colombian] a combination dish of red beans, rice, ground meat, fried sweet plantain, fried pork skin, sausage, avocado, a fried egg, and a corn cake (arepa). Traditionally arranged on a large elliptical platter.

bangers [English] relatively thick, seasoned sausages made with pork, cereal grain, and sometimes beef or veal.

bangus /bong-oose/ [Filipino] variable recipe for popular farm-raised milkfish, commonly stuffed with vegetables or seafood and grilled.

banh pho /bine-(yuh)-fuh/ [Thai, Vietnamese] ribbon-shaped rice noodles.

banh xeo /bine-(yuh)-say-oh/ [Vietnamese] relatively large, crisp, egg and rice-flour crepe or thin pancake, folded over a filling of fresh bean sprouts, cooked mung beans, meat, and shrimp, garnished with fresh herbs, lettuce, and dipping sauce. Diners may use lettuce leaf to roll up and dip crepe pieces with herbs.

banku /bong-koo/ [West African] fermented corn flour and cassava dough mixture, cooked and stirred for a long time in the pot, then formed into quarter-pound balls, popular in Ghana.

baobab /bah-oh-bob/ [West African] the ground or roasted seeds or the pulp of a common African fruit. *also called* **monkey bread.**

bap, bop /bop/ [Korean] steamed rice, often mixed with other grains or beans.

barbari bread [Persian] popular leavened flatbread made with wheat and a little bit of cornmeal, formed into a large round or oblong loaf about the thickness of a person's hand. *see* **nan-e barbari**

barfi *see* **burfi**

barg *see* **kabab-e barg**

bartha *see* **bharta**

baryani *see* **biryani**

basbousa [Middle Eastern] sweet semolina cake topped with almonds and syrup and cut in a diamond pattern. *also* **basbusa, basboosa**

basmati /bahss-mah′-tee/ [Indian] a fragrant, translucent long-grain rice with a delicate nutty flavor.

bastilla *also* **pastilla** [Moroccan] an inverted filo dough pie filled with long-marinated chicken, ground almonds, and spices, with powdered sugar and cinnamon sprinkled on top. These circular pies vary in size from five to sixteen inches in diameter and are cut into wedges and served hot as appetizers to be eaten with a knife and fork. Historically prepared with pigeon meat, now rarely so. *also called* **pigeon pie**

basturma *see* **pastirma**

bati, baati [Indian] grilled wheat-dough balls stuffed with curried potatoes or lentils.

batura *see* **bhatura**

Bauernfrühstück /bow-urn-free-shtik/ [German ("farmer's breakfast")] a fried mixture of eggs, bacon, potato slices, tomatoes, milk, and chives.

bean curd *see* **tofu**

bean thread [Asian] small, transparent noodles made from mung beans or other vegetables. *also called* **cellophane noodles, glass noodles**

béarnaise /bay-ahr-nez/ [French] **1.** a popular sauce characterized by wine vinegar or wine that has been boiled down with tarragon and shallots, combined with butter and egg yolk, lightly cooked. **2.** a style of cooking characterized by the use of béarniase sauce, originally from the Béarn region of SW France. (*Note: foods prepared with lightly cooked eggs may be unsafe for pregnant women, young children, older adults, and those with compromised immune systems.*)

béchamel /bay-shah-mel/ [French (from Louis de Béchamel, 17th century)] a basic white sauce made with butter, flour, and milk or cream, served warm on top of cooked dishes as a custard-like topping. Commonly flavored with nutmeg.

beef Stroganoff [Russian] **1.** common Americanized dish of beef chunks with a mushroom and sour cream sauce, served over noodles. **2.** traditional version of this dish, made with braised beef filet and garnished with chopped dill and parsley, served with potatoes.

beef teriyaki [Japanese] thin strips of beef marinated in teriyaki sauce, then stir-fried or broiled on a skewer.

bee hoon *also* **bihun** /bee-hoon'/ [Indonesian] very thin rice noodles. *see also* **bihun goreng**

beg /beg/ [Ethiopian ("sheep")] lamb.

begendi *see* **hunkar begendi**

begon *see* **baingan**

beignet /ben-yay/ [New Orleans] dough fritter or doughnut sprinkled with powdered sugar, especially popular with coffee at breakfast time.

belacan, belachan /bah-lah-chan/ [Malaysian] *see* **shrimp paste**

belado /bel-ah-doe/ [Indonesian] spicy, made with hot peppers.

Bengali [Indian] a style of cooking from eastern India and Bangladesh characterized by an emphasis on seafood and the frequent use of *panch phoron* (cumin, anise, fenugreek, mustard, and nigella.)

bengan /beng'-on/ [Indian] eggplant. *see also* **baingan**

bengan bartha *see* **baingan bharta**

bento [Japanese ("lunch")] various lunch foods, often accompanied by sauces and artistically presented in a decorated, flat "bento bako" (lunch box). A bento is typically divided into four or five small dishes or compartments.

berbere /bear-beh-ray'/ [Ethiopian] a popular, relatively intense hot spice powder consisting of ground dried red chile peppers and sometimes garlic, salt, and other ingredients. Varies regionally.

beryani *see* **biryani**

besan /bay'-sun/ [Indian] chick pea flour or lentil flour. *also called* **gram flour**

besciamella [Italian] *same as* **béchamel**

beyaynetu /bay-yay'-neh-too/ [Ethiopian] a specified combination or "sampler" of several different prepared foods, served on an injera (sponge bread) platter.

bhaigan *see* **baingan**

bhaji /bah'-jee/ [Indian] **1.** small balls or spoonfuls of chopped vegetables coated with a spiced lentil-flour batter, dropped into hot oil and deep fried. **2.** side dishes, usually mildly spiced fried vegetables. *also* **bhajee**

bhajia /bah'-jee-uh/ **1.** [Indian] small dry-fried snack food morsels. **2.** *(verb)* to fry.

bharta /bahr'-tah/ [Indian] vegetables mashed or cooked to a soft consistency. *also* **bartha, bhurta**

bhat [Nepalese] boiled rice.

bhatura, batura /bah-too'-rah/ [Indian] a puffed-up, deep-fried leavened bread made from refined white flour and sometimes semolina.

bhed s*ee* **bhet**

bhel puri /bell poo'-ree/ [Indian] traditional Bombay snack of puffed rice freshly mixed with cooked lentil squiggles, chopped raw onions, cilantro, tangy chutney, and sometimes tomato, yielding a vividly flavored and textured dish that emits a faint crackling sound.

bhet /bet/ [Thai] duck. *see* **ped**

bhet-yang /bet-yahng/ [Thai] roast duck. *see also* **kang-ped bhet-yang**

bhindi /bin'-dee/ [Indian] okra. *also* **bindi**

bhujia /boo'-jee-uh/ [Indian] Bengali-style fried vegetables.

bhuna /boo'-nuh/ [Indian] a style or stage of cooking characterized by stir-frying curry spice ingredients and vegetables to a carmelized or dry state while adding minimal water, thus yielding a concentrated paste-like gravy. The term may also be loosely applied to describe any dry-fried curry dish.

bhurta *see* **bharta**

bhutuwa [Nepali] fried.

bialy /be-ollie/ [Jewish, named after Bialystock, Poland] a popular flat roll with a bagel-like texture, having a small depression in the top filled with chopped onions.

bibim bap, bibim bop [Korean] a dish of rice and assorted common or exotic vegetables, usually topped with pieces of grilled meat, chile paste, and fried eggs, or sometimes raw eggs. (*Note: foods prepared with raw [i.e., uncooked or unpasteurized] eggs may be unsafe for pregnant women, young children, older adults, and those with compromised immune systems.*)

bibinka, bibingka /bih-bink'-uh/ [Filipino] variable recipe for a popular dessert or snack made from sticky rice, coconut milk, sugar, and tuba (fermented palm-juice) baked on a bed of wilted banana leaves.

Bible tripe [Vietnamese] the lining from the third stomach of a cow or beef, used to augment soup.

bihun goreng /bee-hoon'-go-rheng'/ [Indonesian] stir-fried thin rice noodles (bee hoon) with vegetables and selected meat. *see also* **bee hoon**

biltong [South African] dried beef strips seasoned with coriander and salt.
(*Note: foods prepared with uncooked meat may be unsafe for pregnant women, young children, older adults, and those with compromised immune systems.*)

bindi *see* **bhindi**

bird's-eye chile [various] one of the hottest chile peppers, less than one inch long. *also called* **prik ki nu.**

bird's nest soup [Chinese, other] **1.** a soup made using the expensive, rare harvested nest of a cave-dwelling bird consisting of congealed bird saliva, cooked in chicken broth. **2.** an economical Western adaptation of the original bird's nest soup made using very thin noodles arranged in the shape of a bird's nest or perhaps egg white strands reminiscent of a bird's nest.

birria [Mexican] traditionally, stew made with goat meat or sometimes beef.

biryani /bihr-yah'-nee/ [Indian, other] fancy basmati rice casserole flavored with saffron, meat or vegetable curry, herbs and nuts. *also* **biriani, baryani**

biscotti /bis-cot'-ee/ [Italian] a hard, light, thick-sliced cookie, commonly used for dunking into a coffee beverage.

bissap juice /bee-sop/ [Senegalese] a popular fragrant sweet (iced) tea beverage made from hibiscus flowers, flavored with a mixture of mint, vanilla, lemon, pineapple juice, and other flavors. *also called* **jus de bissap** /jhoo-duh-bee-sop/

bitter leaf *see* **ndole**

bla *see* **pla**

black bean sauce [Chinese] a preparation of fermented black beans with ginger, garlic, rice wine, and other ingredients.

black cake [Jamaican] rich fruitcake made with wine and rum.

blackened [Cajun/New Orleans] a method of cooking (usually fish or chicken) in which the outer layer is seared in a pan with a mixture of Cajun spices, forming a dark-colored outer crust. Typical ingredients include black pepper, white pepper, cayenne pepper, paprika, thyme, oregano, powdered onion, and garlic.

black forest cake [German] a fancy chocolate cake with chocolate and cherry filling and whipped cream frosting garnished with cherries. Made with cherry brandy. *also* **Schwarzwälder Kirschtorte**

blah *see* **pla**

blanched [various] cooked lightly by dipping briefly into boiling water.

blini /blee'-nee/ [Russian] traditional thin plain pancakes to accompany caviar (or sometimes smoked salmon) served warm with sour cream or butter and rolled up and eaten by hand or with a fork and knife. Can also be eaten with honey or jam, more like a dessert. *also* **bliny, blinis**

blintz [Jewish, other] a very thin, sweet wheat-flour pancake wrapped around a filling of sweetened cottage cheese, fruit, chicken, or chocolate. Usually pan-fried and served warm, accompanied by applesauce or sour cream.

blood sausage [various] sausage made from blood and meat fat, usually with a cereal filler.

blowfish *see* **fugu**

Blutwurst /bloot´-voorsht/ [German] spicy salty blood sausage.

bo /bahw/ [Vietnamese] beef.

bobo de camarão /baw-baw-day-cah´-mah-rau´/ [Brazilian] popular Bahia stew of shrimp and yuca puree, with tomato, cilantro, onion, coconut milk, and palm oil, sometimes with chile peppers or cashews and peanuts.

bobotie /bah-boo´-tee/ [South African] a traditional curry-flavored baked meat loaf made with lamb or beef, soaked bread pieces, fruits, vegetables, chutney, and sometimes raisins and almonds, all topped with an egg custard.

Bockwurst /bock´-vursht/ [German] a veal sausage made with egg, milk, chives, parsley, and sometimes pork, traditionally consumed with bock beer.

boerewors /boor-uh-vorse/ [South African] traditional spiced beef and pork sausage.

bok choy [Chinese] a mild-flavored vegetable similar to celery, with broad, dark, edible leaves.

bokum /bo-kuhm/ [Korean] stir-fry.

bolani *see* **boolawnee**

bolillo /bo-lee´-oh/ [Mexican] a small sandwich roll.

bolinho de bacalhau /bo-lean´-yo-deh-bah´-kah-lao/ [Brazilian] popular appetizer of fried codfish croquettes served with a sauce.

bolo de milho /bo´-lo-duh-meal´-yo/ [Brazilian] slightly leavened sweet corn cake made with milk and eggs, served warm or at room temperature.

Bolognese /bo-lo-nay´-say/ [Italian] classic pasta sauce made with meat, tomatoes, and rich seasonings.

bondas [Indian] battered and fried balls (croquettes) of mashed potatoes, lentil flour, and seasonings.

boolawnee /boo-lah-nee/ [Afghan] fried or clay-oven-baked pastries filled with chopped leeks, scallions, and seasoning, sometimes with potato. *also* **bulanee, boulanee, bolani**

bop *see* **bap**

bordelaise /bohr-duh-lez/ [French] a rich brown sauce made with butter, shallots, bone marrow, red wine, and seasonings.

borek /beu-rehk/ [Turkish ("pastry")] filo dough pastry in variously shaped packets stuffed with cheese, spinach, or sometimes meats, either baked or fried. *also* **börek, burek, bourek, boregi**

borscht [Russian, other] **1.** popular dark red beet soup, made with vegetables and typically fortified with meat, cooked with vinegar and usually served hot with a spoonful of sour cream. **2.** one of a number of similar versions of borscht, which are vegetarian or are served cold. **3.** a hot soup made with cabbage and tomato. *also* **borsch, borshch**

boti [Indian] **1.** cubes or chunks of marinated meat. **2.** a traditional chopping instrument.

Bouchée à la Reine /boo-shay-ah-lah-renn/ [French ("mouthful for the queen")] fancy puff pastry filled with diced chicken and mushrooms, laden with rich sauce (usually béchamel). Sometimes made with sweetbreads.

boudin noir /boo-denh-nwar/ [French] blood sausage.

bouillabaisse /boo-ya-bez/ [French, from Provence] a vernacular recipe for richly flavored fish soup or stew, typically prepared with chunks of ordinary fish, garden vegetables, herbs and spices, white wine, shrimp, and other seafood. Traditionally served with croutons and aioli on the side.

boulanee *see* **boolawnee**

bouranee badenjan *see* **buranee badenjan**

bourek *see* **borek**

bozena shuro /boʹ-zeh-nuh-shooʹ-ro/ [Ethiopian] a popular stew of powdered split peas or beans cooked in butter, typically combined with chopped beef or other ingredients and seasoned with berbere (hot spice).

bplah *see* **pla**

braised [various] slow-cooked in a sealed container with very little water.

brasa, a la [Latin American] cooked on an open charcoal grill.

Bratwurst /brahtʹ-voorsht/ [German] seasoned curved sausage made with veal, pork, ginger, and nutmeg.

breadfruit [various] moderately large, loaf-shaped tropical fruit found in the Pacific region and other areas, having a sweet-smelling starchy flesh.

bresaola /breh-zohlʹ-uh/ [Italian] air-cured dry raw beef, typically served thin-sliced as an appetizer with lemon juice and oil.
(*Note: foods prepared with raw meat may be unsafe for pregnant women, young children, older adults, and those with compromised immune systems.*)

brie /bree/ [French] a soft yellowish-white cheese with a firm whitish rind, made into a wheel about 6-12 inches in diameter, commonly served in

wedge-shaped slices with bread and wine.
(*Note: government food safety experts advise pregnant women, older adults, and those with compromised immune systems not to eat brie unless it is labeled as made with pasteurized milk.*)

brioche /bree-oh-sh/ [French] a fancy sweet butter-and-egg bread or roll baked in a special molded pan with fluted sides.

brisket [various] the breast portion of beef adjacent to the foreleg.

briwat /bree-watt/ [Moroccan] a small triangle-shaped filo-dough pastry with a meat, vegetable, fish, or fruit filling.

brochette /bro-shett/ [French, other] pieces of meat or seafood cooked on a small skewer.

brown sauce 1. [Chinese] a common sauce made with beef broth, oyster sauce, soy sauce, cornstarch, and sugar. **2.** [French] a traditional culinary "mother sauce" made from a variable mixture of butter, beef broth, herbs, vegetables, pepper, flour or cornstarch, and other ingredients. *also called* **espagnole 3.** one of several traditional brown sauces made from beef or veal bones, including fond de veau, espagnole, and demi-glace.

brown stew [Jamaican] a popular method of marinating, lightly frying, and then stewing chicken or fish with onions, garlic, tomatoes, green pepper, and spices.

Brunswick stew [various, derived from Native American] **1.** a traditional game meat (squirrel) stew, now generally made instead with slow-cooked chicken, corn, lima beans, and other chopped vegetables. **2.** a vernacular name for a stew created by combining whatever inexpensive meat and vegetable ingredients happen to be readily available at a given time.

bruschetta /broo-skett-uh/ [Italian] oven-toasted, day-old bread slices, typically topped with tomato, garlic, herb seasoning, and olive oil.

bu [Thai] crab.

bucatini [Italian] hollow spaghetti.

bûche de Nöel /byoosh-duh-no-el/ [French] yule-log rolled cake with a cream filling and butter frosting. Commonly chocolate and mocha flavored, but almond, vanilla, or other flavors may be found.

Buddha's delight *or* **Buddhist delight** [Chinese] a common vegetarian preparation of tofu chunks, black mushrooms, and mixed vegetables cooked in brown sauce, preferred for Chinese New Year and other holidays.

Buddhist vegetables [Chinese] mixed vegetables including lotus root.

bulanee *see* **boolawnee**

bulanee katchalu /boo-lah-knee-kah-chah-loo/ [Afghan] fried pastries filled with mashed potatoes, ground meat, and seasonings.

bulgogi /bull-go-kee/ [Korean] marinated rib-eye beef sliced thin, often cooked on a tabletop grill, typically served as "ssam" (to be rolled up by the diner in a lettuce leaf, along with various vegetables, rice, and a hot-pepper soybean paste, and eaten.) *also* **bul ko ki, pulgogi**

bulgur wheat [Turkish, other] parboiled cracked wheat with a pleasant chewy texture. *also* **bulgar, bulghur, burghol**

bun [Vietnamese] thin rice vermicelli.

Bundt pan [German] a decoratively-shaped cake pan with a raised cone in the center, used for making an upside-down cake called a Bundt cake.

bunuelos /boo-nyueh′-loce/ [Mexican, other] thin, broad cookies or fritters made with cheese and corn, commonly served with syrup and cinnamon. *also* **buñuelos**

buranee badenjan /boo-rah′-nee-bah-den-john/ [Afghan] eggplant stew with yogurt and meat sauce.

buranee kadu /boo-rah′-nee-kah-doo/ [Afghan] pumpkin stew with yogurt and meat sauce.

burek *see* **borek**

burfi [Indian] a sweet dessert similar to fudge made with sugar and milk powder, cooked with ground fruit, nut, or vegetable paste, cooled and solidified and typically cut into squares.

burghol *see* **bulgur wheat**

burrito [Tex-Mex] a large soft flour tortilla wrapped around a filling of meat or beans and optional vegetables, such as shredded lettuce, diced tomato, onions, and salsa, often sprinkled with shredded cheddar cheese. May sometimes include rice, cilantro, sour cream, guacamole, and other ingredients.

butter chicken [Indian] marinated chicken pieces usually roasted in a tandoor (clay oven) and finished with a richly seasoned butter-tomato sauce. *see* **chicken tikka makhani.**

butter tea [Tibetan] traditional hot tea thoroughly blended with a little butter, salt, and milk.

C

caakiri *see* **tiakri**

cabanossi [Central and Southern European] pork and beef smoked sausage flavored with garlic, similar to salami.
(*Note: government food safety experts advise heating all deli meats or luncheon meats to steaming hot before they are eaten by pregnant women, young children, older adults, or those with compromised immune systems.*)

cacciatore /kah-chah-tor'-eh *anglicized*: catch a tory/ [Italian ("hunter's style")] **1.** meat (usually chicken) stewed in a rich sauce of tomatoes, onions, herbs, and wine, typically with green peppers and mushrooms. **2.** a loosely-applied term designating a dish to have "hunter's style" characteristics.

cacik /juh'-jehk/ [Turkish] a popular yogurt and chopped cucumber preparation, served as an appetizer, a dip, or as a side dish with kebabs.

cactus [Mexican] the edible arms or fruit of the prickly pear or saguaro cactus.

Caesar salad [Italian-American (after Caesar Cardini, chef)] a salad made with romaine lettuce, croutons, and a special dressing containing garlic, black pepper, Worcestershire sauce, Parmesan cheese, and sometimes raw egg.
(*Note: foods prepared with raw [i.e., uncooked or unpasteurized] eggs may be unsafe for pregnant women, young children, older adults, and those with compromised immune systems.*)

Cajun /kay'-jn/ [New Orleans] the vernacular cuisine of descendants of French-Canadians deported from Acadia (Nova Scotia) who resettled in Louisiana, characterized by seafood stews, sharp spices, and a prevalence of rice with prepared dishes.

calabaza /kah-lah-bah'-sah/ [Mexican, other] pumpkin, usually a green-colored variety.

calaloo [Caribbean] a leafy green vegetable somewhat similar to spinach, commonly sautéed.

calalu [West African] **1.** a variable stew of spinach or other greens, various meats, seafood, and salt fish. **2.** the edible leaves of various agricultural plants, such as amaranth, manioc, or taro. *also* **calalou, kallaloo**

calamari [Italian, other] squid, usually fried.

caldereta /call-deer-ree'-tah/ [Filipino] goat stew made in a spicy tomato base.

caldo /call'-doe/ *or* **caldi** /call'-dee/ **1.** [Italian] hot. **2.** [Spanish] broth.

caldo gallego /call'-doe-gahl-yay'-go/ [Spanish] a casserole of potatoes, beans, greens, and pork.

caldo verde /call'-doe-vair'-deh/ [Potuguese ("green soup")] a kettle of potatoes, leafy greens, beans, and sometimes sausage.

California rolls [Japanese] rolls of sushi rice, real or imitation crabmeat, avocado, cucumber, and sometimes fish roe, wrapped in edible seaweed and cut into slices. Sometimes rolled "inside out" so that the rice layer is on the outside and the seaweed is concealed. *see* **sushi**

calzone /cal-zoh'-neh *commonly mispronounced* cal-zone'/ [Italian] a type of pizza with the dough folded over and sealed, so that the toppings are enclosed as a filling. *similar to* **stromboli**

camarão à paulista /kah-mah-rao'-ah-po-lees'-tah/ [Brazilian] Sao-Paulo style sautéed mari-

nated jumbo shrimp with garlic, olive oil, and
cilantro.

camarones /kah-mah-roh′-ness/ [Spanish]
shrimp, prawn.

Camembert /cam-maum-bare/ [French] a soft,
yellowish-white cheese with a firm whitish rind,
formed in small (4-5 in.) wheels and commonly
cut into wedge-shaped pieces and eaten with
bread or crackers.
(*Note: government food safety experts advise
pregnant women, older adults, and those with
compromised immune systems not to eat soft
cheeses such as Camembert unless they are labeled as made with pasteurized milk.*

campur /chomm′-poor/ [Indonesian] mixed, mixture.

canapé /kah-nah-pay/ [French ("sofa")] a tiny appetizer consisting of a piece of bread, toast, or
cracker topped with a bit of cheese, caviar, or
other delicious topping.

canard /kah-nahr/ [French] duck.

cannellini [Italian] large white kidney beans.

cannelloni [Italian] large cylindrical noodles
stuffed with a filling and baked.

cannoli [Italian] thin, cylindrical cookies, filled
with a sweet ricotta cheese mixture flavored with
candied fruit and cocoa.

Cantonese [Chinese] a sophisticated style of
southern Chinese cooking from the Canton
(Guangdong) region, characterized by subtle
seasonings which enhance the delicate natural
flavor of the ingredients.

capers [various] small, pickled, edible buds of
the caper shrub, which have a strong flavor.

capocollo /kah-po-kohl′-oh/ [Italian] smoked salt pork, usually sliced thin and eaten raw as an appetizer.
(*Note: foods prepared with raw meat may be unsafe for pregnant women, young children, older adults, and those with compromised immune systems.*)

cappellini [Italian] angel-hair (very thin) pasta.

capsaicin /cap-say′-sin/ burning ingredient in hot chile peppers.

capsicums [English, other] peppers.

carbon *see* **al carbon**

carbonara [Italian] creamy pasta sauce made with bacon or ham, cheese, and sometimes raw or partially cooked egg yolk.
(*Note: foods prepared with raw [i.e., uncooked or unpasteurized] eggs may be unsafe for pregnant women, young children, older adults, and those with compromised immune systems.*)

carne /car-nay/ [Spanish, other] meat.

carne asada [Mexican, other ("roast meat")] **1.** marinated beef barbecued on a grill (traditionally over an open pit) then served in carved chunks alongside chopped onions and salsa, all rolled up in tortillas by the diner and eaten. **2.** an event at which carne asada is prepared and served.

carne-de-sol /kahr′-neh-day-sol′/ [Brazilian] dried beef marinated with kosher salt and sun-dried.

carne seca /kahr′-neh-say′-kah/ [Brazilian, other] dried beef strips, somewhat similar to jerky.
(*Note: foods prepared with uncooked meat may be unsafe for pregnant women, young children, older adults, and those with compromised im-*

mune systems.)

carpaccio /car-pot′-she-oh/ [Italian] very thin-sliced raw beef or tuna, topped with olive oil, lemon juice, mustard sauce, and other garnishes, served as an appetizer.

(*Note: foods prepared with raw meat or fish may be unsafe for pregnant women, young children, older adults and those with compromised immune systems.*)

casquinha de siri /kas-keen′-yah-day-see′-ree/ [Brazilian] crab meat sautéed with cilantro, tomato, scallions, green pepper, and coconut milk, traditionally served in an empty crab shell or scallop shell, topped with roasted cassava meal or bread crumbs.

cassava [various] **1.** a fleshy, bitter (detoxified) or mild tropical tuber, native to South America, pounded into flour or prepared as a side dish. **2.** cassava leaf. *also called* **manioc** /man-yock/, **yuca** /yoo-kah/

cassava leaf [various] reputedly medicinal leafy greens of the cassava (manioc) plant, used in stews, for example with fish or meat. *see also* **calalu**

cassoulet /kah-soo-lay/ [French] traditional slow-cooked casserole with white beans, sausage, and duck, goose, or pork, topped with bread crumbs.

cayenne pepper /kye-enn′/ [various] an extremely hot spice made from skinny red chile peppers, which are dried and ground into powder.

ceebu jën *see* **thiebou dieun**

cellophane noodles [Asian] small, transparent noodles made from mung beans or other vegetables. *also called* **bean thread, glass noodles, harusame, woon sen, mien**

cepelinai [Lithuanian] potato balls filled with meat or cheese.

cerkez tavugu /chek-hez-tah-vuhk/ [Turkish ("Circassian chicken" named after a Turkish ethnic group originating in central Asia.)] chicken with a sauce made from finely chopped nuts, served at room temperature. *also* **cerkez tavuk, çerkez tavugu**

cerveza /sair-vay'-sah/ [Mexican] beer.

ceviche *also* **seviche** /seh-veech'-eh/ [Latin American] an appetizer made from raw seafood marinated in hot chiles, onions, tomatoes, and lime juice. Exact preparation varies by region. (*Note: foods prepared with raw seafood may be unsafe for pregnant women, young children, older adults, and those with compromised immune systems.*)

chaat, chat /chott/ [Indian ("snack")] name for any snack, often prepared with seasoning including spicy and tangy flavors. For example, fruit chaat, papri chaat.

chaat masala [Indian] a spice mixture used to season snacks, often incorporating coriander, cumin, amchoor (mango powder), and black rock salt.

cha gio /chah-zaaw/ [Vietnamese] deep-fried crispy spring rolls, made from ground pork, seafood, bean thread, and chopped vegetables, all rolled together in a thin "rice paper" wrapper. Typically served with mint, cilantro, and cucumber and eaten by wrapping in a lettuce leaf and dipping in a fish-flavored sauce. *also called* **spring rolls, imperial rolls**

chai [Indian (from Chinese *char)*] tea.

chakli, chakri [Indian] squiggles of flavored rice dough pressed through a special ricer and deep fried. A popular Southern Indian snack.

chalau [Afghan] white basmati rice, usually with cumin and cinnamon, typically accompanied by side items, such as spinach or pumpkin stew. *also* **chalaw, challaw**

challah /hghah'-luh *also* hah'-luh/ [Jewish] traditional sweet, braided bread made with egg, eaten especially on the Sabbath. *also* **hallah**

chalupas /chah-loo-pah/ [Mexican ("canoes")] beans or meat with toppings piled in special boat-shaped tortillas or simply on a bed of chips.

champignon /shohn-peen-yohn/ [French] mushrooms.

champurrado [Mexican] thick, chocolate-flavored atole (hot corn flour beverage).

chana, **channa** /chah-nah/ [Indian] chick peas, not to be confused with chhena (cottage cheese). *see* **chole**

chana dal /chah-nah-dahl/ [Indian] split yellow lentils.

chana masala [Indian] chick peas cooked in a sauce with an onion, garlic, and mixed spices.

chapati, chapatti /chah-pah'-tee/ [Indian/Pakistani] popular thin, unleavened flat wheat bread cooked in a dry skillet and sometimes briefly puffed up over the heat of an open flame. *see* **roti**

chap jae, chap chae [Korean] *see* **chop chae**

chapli kabab [Pakistani] small morsels of finely ground meat mixed with spices and other ingredients and pan-fried as patties, similar to a hamburger. Predominant seasonings are coriander and red pepper.

char kway teow [Malaysia] popular street food made of fried broad rice noodles, eggs, soy sauce, bean sprouts, and seafood or meats.

char siu bao /chah-shwee-bow/ [Chinese] baked or steamed buns filled with barbecued pork. *also* **cha siu bao, cha siu bow, cha sui bao**

chat *see* **chaat**

Chateaubriand /shah-toe-bree-ohn/ [French] **1.** large, log-shaped chunk of a select filet of beef with the fat trimmed off, seasoned with coarsely-ground pepper and simple flavorings, cooked rare in butter and covered with a sauce, then carved into thin slices for eating. **2.** a style of cooking similar to Chateaubriand, but with different meats.

chebjen *see* **thiebou dieun**

chelo, chelow [Persian] rice that is carefully prepared and steamed, without other ingredients. *see also* **polo**

chelo kabab [Persian] lamb long-marinated in onion juice and yogurt, then broiled on a skewer, served alongside accompanying saffron-flavored rice, sometimes topped with raw egg.
(*Note: foods prepared with raw [i.e., uncooked or unpasteurized] eggs may be unsafe for pregnant women, young children, older adults, and those with compromised immune systems.*)

chenna, chhana [Indian] freshly made cheese curds used in some dessert recipes or to make paneer.

chevre /shev′-ruh/ [French] goat cheese, of various shapes and textures, served by itself or as an ingredient in other foods.

chhana *see* **chenna**

chhole /cho′-lay/ [Indian] chick peas. *see* **chole**

chhwela *see* **chwela**

Chiang Mai [Thai] recipes characteristic of the city of Chiang Mai in northwest Thailand, commonly using a red curry sauce with peanut and coconut milk.

chicharron /chee-chah-rohn′/ [Latin American, Filipino] fried pork skin or shoulder. *plural* **chicharrones**

chicken curry [Indian] generic name for chicken stew cooked with onions, garlic, ginger, spices, and tomato.

chicken fettuccine Alfredo [Italian] popular combination of chicken and pasta with heavy cream sauce. May contain raw egg.
(Note: foods prepared with raw [i.e., uncooked or unpasteurized] eggs may be unsafe for pregnant women, young children, older adults, and those with compromised immune systems.)

chicken karahi [Indian, Pakistani] chicken pieces cooked in a karahi (wok-like pan) with tomatoes, onions, ginger, peppers, herbs, and spices, originally from the Northwest Frontier area of the subcontinent.

chicken Kiev [Russian] a wrap of thinly-pounded chicken breast meat, pinched closed around an herb-butter mixture, then battered and fried. When the dish is served, the chicken must be punctured carefully to control the boiling butter that squirts out.

chicken Madras /mah-drahss/ [Indian-style, named after a city] **1.** British term for chicken with hot spicy pepper seasoning. **2.** chicken prepared with mustard seed, coconut, and curry leaf.

chicken masala [Indian] marinated chicken pieces simmered in a thick sauce of onions, spices, tomato, and yogurt.

chicken pakora [Indian] deep-fried chicken fritters made with a chickpea or lentil flour batter, typically an appetizer.

chicken sekuwa [Nepalese] barbecued marinated chicken breast with ginger, garlic, and spices.

chicken shaslik [Indian, other] chunks of chicken typically grilled on a skewer with tomatoes, onions, and green peppers.

chicken tikka /tih'-kah/ [Indian] pieces of marinated boneless chicken or chicken breast, typically cooked with mild spices.

chicken tikka makhani, chicken tikka makhanwala [Indian] chunks of boneless chicken or chicken breast, marinated and usually roasted on a skewer, then served in a spiced tomato and butter sauce. *see* **butter chicken**

chicken tikka masala [Indian-style dish originating in the U.K.] chunks of marinated boneless chicken or chicken breast, usually roasted on a skewer, then served in a spicy tomato, onion, and yogurt-based sauce.

chigae /chig'-ay/ [Korean] traditional hot soup or stew of various mixed ingredients. *also* **jigae, jjigae, tchigae**

chilaquiles /chee-lah-kee'-les/ [Mexican ("poor man's food")] strips of stale tortillas, either made into a casserole with tomato sauce and cheese (sometimes with chicken) or mixed with scrambled eggs, or just covered with sauce, popular for breakfast.

chile /chilly/ hot pepper. *plural* **chiles** /chillies/

chile rellenos /chilly ray-yay′-noce/ [Mexican] a preparation of select (usually large) chile peppers stuffed with cheese, then coated liberally with an egg batter and fried (or baked). Usually topped with salsa.

chili powder [various] a spice mixture consisting of ground dried chiles and other spices.

chimichanga [Tex-Mex] rolled or folded tortilla pouch filled with meat, cheese, vegetables, and seasonings, then deep fried.

chimichurri [Latin American] popular barbecue sauce made with olive oil, garlic, herbs, spices, and lemon juice or vinegar.

Chinese sausage [Chinese, other] a lightly salted sausage made of duck's liver or pork, which is cooked, sliced, and added to other dishes.

Chinese spice [Chinese, Southeast Asian] a variable combination of star anise, cinnamon, and other spices. *see* **five-spice**

chipotle /chip-oat′-lay/ [Mexican] dried, smoked jalapeno peppers, with a smoky, sweet taste, commonly made into a richly-flavored hot sauce.

chitterlings, chit'lins /chit′-linz/ [Southern/Soul food] pork small intestines, cleaned thoroughly and boiled for many hours, with chunks of onion, celery, seasoning, and vinegar typically added, cooked down in its own juices. Served as a lunch or dinner main dish.

cho cho beef [Chinese] sautéed beef on a skewer.

chole, chhole /cho′-lay/ [Indian] chick pea stew commonly prepared with tomatoes, ginger, garlic, and curry spices. Sometimes mixed with potatoes (**aloo chole**).

cholent /choln't/ [Jewish ("warm")] slow-cooked stew of kosher meat, beans, barley, and vegetables, a traditional Sabbath meal.

chop chae /cheb-chay/ [Korean] stir-fried transparent noodles and mixed vegetables with soy sauce, garlic, sesame oil, sugar, and sometimes meat. Usually served with kim chi and rice. *also* **chap chae, jap che, japchae, chap jae** *see also* **cellophane noodles**

chop suey, chop sui [Chinese (from Cantonese, *tsap seui* "mixed pieces")] Americanized Chinese dish of small pieces of meat and vegetables (for example bok choy, celery, mushrooms, water chestnuts, and bell pepper) stir-fried and served over rice.

chorizo /cho-ree'-so/ [Spanish, Latin American ("sausage")] a hard, often spicy sausage made with chopped pork, paprika, garlic, and other spices, eaten whole or cut into pieces and added to other dishes.

choun la [Newar] term for ground meat, as spoken in Kathmandu area.

chow /ch'-ow/ [Ethiopian] salt.

chow [Chinese] stir-fried food.

chow foon, chow fun [Chinese] large, flat, soft fried noodles cooked with vegetables or meat.

chow gai kew [Chinese] large-sized chunks of chicken stir-fried with mixed vegetables.

chow har kew [Chinese] fried jumbo shrimp with mixed vegetables.

chow mei fun, chow mai fun [Chinese] thin rice noodles, stir-fried.

chow mein [Chinese] a meat or vegetable preparation including onions, bamboo shoots, celery, and mushrooms, served over crispy noodles.

choyla *see* **chwela**

chrin *see* **hrin**

chuletas /choo-let′-us/ [Latin American] pork chops.

churrascaria /shoo-hah′-skah-ree′-ah/ [Brazilian ("barbecue house")] a restaurant specializing in grilled meats, with all-you-can-eat rounds of rodizio and a salad bar.

churrasco /shoo-hah′-sko/ [Brazilian] a barbecue of grilled meats prepared with salt and sometimes garlic, but no barbecue sauce.

churrasquinhos /shoo-hah-skeen′-yose/ [Brazilian] dishes prepared with small skewers, such as grilled pieces of meat, chicken, shrimp, or sausage, very popular in Brazil with street vendors.

churros [Spanish, Mexican] deep-fried extruded-dough fritters with fluted striations, comparable to doughnuts in stick form, rolled in sugar and consumed as a breakfast or snack with a hot beverage. Variations may include a filling in the middle or a sprinkling of cinnamon.

chutney [Indian] variable condiment combining fruits or vegetables, vinegar, sugar, and spices, usually with a potent flavor combining hot, sour, salty, and sweet ingredients, used to enhance or supplement various dishes.

chwela /chway′-lah/ [Newar] term for barbecued or marinated roasted meat of the Kathmandu region of Nepal. *also* **chhwela, chwyela, choyla**, *other spellings*

cilantro [various] fresh coriander leaf, a popular sweet fragrant herb, also known as Chinese parsley.

civet /see-vay/ [French, Italian] hare or other game meat traditionally stewed in animal blood and wine sauce.

clay pot [Chinese, other] a prepared dish that is placed into a small earthenware vessel, typically with a lid, and baked in an oven. It is then served at the table in the clay vessel, which is typically too hot to touch.

Cleopatra chicken [European] chicken breast with capers, onions, and wine sauce.

coco bread [Jamaican] a cake-like bread made with grated coconut.

coconut milk [various] a creamy liquid produced by pressing grated fresh coconut meat. Not related to the liquid that is naturally found inside a coconut.

coconut water [various] the liquid that is naturally found inside a coconut.

cocoyam *see* **taro**

comida /co-mee´-dah/ [Spanish] food or meal.

compote /kahm-pote/ [French, other] fruit slow-cooked in sugar syrup.

con [Spanish, Italian] with.

con carne /con-car´-nay/ [Spanish] with meat.

condensed milk [various] a type of evaporated milk with sugar added.

confit /cun-feet/ [French] salted meat or poultry cooked and preserved in its own fat or juices.

congee [Chinese] rice soup or porridge consumed for breakfast, often with bits of meat, nuts, or other garnishes.

conkies [Caribbean] sweet vegetable and fruit dumplings steamed in plantain leaves or banana leaves, Barbados-style.

con queso /con-kay′-so/ [Mexican] with cheese.

consommé /con-suh-may/ [French] a clarified soup heavily enriched with meat and vegetable flavorings, served hot or cold.

coo coo *also* **cou cou** [Barbadian] corn meal paste cooked with okra, typically served with steamed flying fish.

coq au vin /kuhk-oh-venh/ [French] chicken slow-cooked in wine.

coquilles Saint-Jacques /co-key-senh-jhak/ [French] scallops cooked in a wine-flavored gravy, lightly baked in the half shell.

cordon bleu [French] boneless chicken breast pounded flat and rolled up with thin-sliced Swiss cheese and ham, breaded and baked.

corned beef [various] beef that has been preserved with salt.

cotto [Italian] **1.** cooked. **2.** cooked ham. *see* **prosciutto cotto**

cou cou *see* **coo coo**

couscous *also* **cous cous** /koose-koose/ [African, other] tiny spherical pasta granules, usually made from semolina flour, cooked and added to other foods such as stews.

coxinha de galinha /co-sheen′-yuh-deh-gah-lean′-yuh/ [Brazilian] popular snack of chicken croquettes.

crab Rangoon [U.S. origin] appetizer sometimes served in Chinese restaurants, consisting of crabmeat, cream cheese, garlic, onion, and soy sauce wrapped in wonton "envelopes" and deep fried.

crème brûlée /crem-broo-lay/ [French] baked custard with a torch-melted sugar glaze on top, served chilled as a dessert.

Creole sauce [Cajun/Creole] a spicy tomato-based sauce including peppers, onions, and Cajun seasonings, used with meat, seafood, and rice dishes.

crêpes /krepp/ [French] very thin pancakes, commonly eaten rolled up with other foods or sweetened. Originally from Brittany region in northwest France. *singular* **crêpe**

crispy [Chinese] **1.** coated with a bread-crumb egg batter and baked or fried to a crisp. **2.** meat items twice-cooked, for example baked then deep fried, so that the interior is well-done and tender while the exterior is crisp. **3.** [Thai, other] deep fried to a crisp state.

croquetas /crow-ket-us/ [Cuban, Spanish, other] croquettes.

crudités /croo-dee-tay/ [French] **1.** raw vegetables (sometimes blanched) usually cut into smallish pieces, placed in a colorful arrangement and served cold as an appetizer. **2.** common Americanized version of crudités served with a creamy dip as a party platter.

crudo, cruda [Italian] raw.

Cuban sandwich [Cuba and Florida] a popular toasted sandwich made with an eight-inch long roll split lengthwise, containing thin slices of ham, roast pork, and Swiss cheese, plus pickles, mayonnaise, and mustard.

cucumber raita /rye-tuh/ [Indian] cucumber yogurt dressing or sauce. *see* **raita**

curry, curried [various] foods prepared with a characteristic family of aromatic, flavorful herb and spice blends of South Asian origin, or the spice mixtures themselves when used in combination with such dishes. Curry-type seasonings, which are also popular in East Asia and in West Indian and South African recipes, are highly variable and range in "hotness" from mild to very intense. Although there is a culinary herb called the curry plant, which has fragrant leaves that smell and taste similar to curry seasonings, this is not normally what is being referred to as "curry" in prepared dishes. *Curried* means prepared using curry-type spice and herb mixtures. *see also following entries*

curry [Chinese] a dish prepared with a spice mixture similar to Indian curry, with somewhat more emphasis on mustard seed.

curry [Indian (from Tamil *kari* "sauce" or other sources)] **1.** a food or stew cooked with a variable blend of prepared spices, resulting in a highly flavorful and aromatic dish, most commonly incorporating coriander, turmeric, cumin, and chiles, and usually ginger, garlic, and many additional spices, such as fenugreek, cinnamon, cloves, black pepper, cardamom, and mustard, and sometimes yogurt. **2.** colloquial term for Indian food.

curry [Thai] dishes prepared with one of a number of variable hot or mild curry spice mixtures. *see* **red curry, green curry, Massaman curry, Panang curry, yellow curry.**

curry powder [various] a pre-mixed combination of several dried powdered spices, usually including coriander, turmeric, cumin, chile, fenugreek, and other ingredients, available in grocery stores.

curry puff [Malaysian, other] flaky baked dumplings made with two types of dough, stuffed with curried potato, onion, and chopped meat.

curry sauce [various] a sauce derived from curry spices cooked with vegetables and herbs, commonly garlic, onions or scallions, tomatoes, fresh ginger or other ingredients, and sometimes yogurt or cream.

curtido [Salvadoran] traditional pickled cabbage, similar to coleslaw, typically used as a topping for pupusas.

D

daal *see* **dal**

dabo /dah-bo/ [Ethiopian] bread cooked in a large raised loaf, originally for the Sabbath.

daegu [Korean] codfish. *also* **dae ku**

daging /dah-khing'/ [Indonesian, Malaysian] meat. *also* **daging babi** pork meat **daging ayam** chicken meat **daging sapi** beef.

dahi [Indian] yogurt.

dahi vada /dah-hee-vah-dah/ *also* **dahi bhalla** /dah-hee-vah-lah/ [Indian] lentil-flour dumplings dipped in yogurt, served with chutney.

dahl *see* **dal**

daikon [Japanese] a large, white sweet radish in the turnip family, commonly added to salads or stir-fried, or grated and used in dipping sauce.

dak /duck/ [Korean] chicken.

dak gui /duck-gwee/ [Korean] marinated chicken, which may be grilled at the table and served "ssam" style. *see also* **ssam**

dal /dahl/ [Indian] **1.** a prepared dish of curried cooked lentils or other legumes, including beans or split peas, having a soupy or stew-like consistency. **2.** the various lentil or other ingredients used in dal. *also* **daal, dhal, dahl**

dal makhani [Indian] black lentils and red kidney beans cooked in a butter-cream curry sauce with tomato, ginger, herbs, and spices.

dal soup [Indian] curried lentil soup.

dan dan mein, dan dan noodles [Chinese] thin egg noodles topped with a spicy Szechuan peanut (or sesame) sauce, sometimes with chicken or pork included. *also* **den den**

debe, dibi [Senegalese] grilled marinated meat or fish with onion and mustard sauce.

dendé /den′-day/ [various] African palm oil with a reddish color, popular in Bahia recipes.

den den *see* **dan dan**

derma *see* **kishke**

dhal *see* **dal**

dhansak /dahn-sahk/ [Indian] a sweet-and-sour curry, traditionally combining several types of lentils in the same dish and incorporating various meat or vegetable ingredients. A specialty of the Parsi ethnic-religious group.

dhingri, dingri [Indian] mushrooms.

dibi *see* **debe**

dim sum [Chinese ("dot hearts")] traditional brunch consisting of small portions of varied offerings, typically presented in restaurants on wheeled carts or trays, including steamed and fried dumplings, meat, vegetable and seafood preparations, and rice balls.

ding [Chinese] toasted almonds.

dingri [Indian] mushrooms. *also* **dhingri**

dinorado /dee-noh-rah′-doh/ [Filipino] a fancy reddish-colored mountain-grown rice having a nutty flavor, served on special occasions.

dinuguan /dee-noo-goo′-ahn/ [Filipino] popular stew made with pork, pork blood, tuba (palm flower) vinegar, and sometimes intestine. *also called* "chocolate pork."

djolof rice *see* **jollof rice**

dock [various] a bitter plant similar to buckwheat.

doenjang /den-jahng/ [Korean] fermented soy bean paste, similar to miso. *also* **dwen jang, toenjang**

doenjang jjigae /den-jahng-chig-ay/ [Korean] traditional stew made with soybean paste. *also* **dwen jang chigae,** *many other spellings*

dolma 1. [Turkish] stuffed vegetables or a food with a filling of some kind. **2.** [Greek, other] *see* **dolmades**

dolmades /dol-mah′-dess/ *also* **dolmathes** /dol-mah′-thees/ [Greek, Middle Eastern] **1.** stuffed grape leaves, wrapped around a filling of rice, ground meat, and olive oil, typically with garlic, onion, herbs, and lemon flavor, served hot. **2.** a vegetarian version of grape leaves stuffed with rice, olive oil, and other ingredients, typically served at room temperature.

dolmeh /dole-may′/ [Persian] various vegetables stuffed with seasoned ground meat and rice.

doner kebab /doeh-nehr-kah-bob/ [Turkish, Middle Eastern, other] a large cylindrical stack of sliced and ground lamb grilled on a spit, then shaved into thin slices. *similar to* **gyro**

doogh *also* **dugh** /doohg/ [Persian, Middle Eastern] mint-flavored yogurt beverage with a cottage-cheese taste.

dopiaza /doe-pyah′-zuh/ [Indian ("two onions")] meat recipe with extra onions added at two stages, for example cooked into an onion sauce, then garnished with scallions. *also* **dupiaza, doh peeazah**

doro /do-ro/ [Ethiopian ("hen")] chicken.

doro wat /do-ro-wutt/ [Ethiopian] chicken sautéed in butter with onions and berbere (hot pepper seasoning) usually topped with a hard-boiled egg. *also* **dorowat**

dosa /doe′-sah/ [South Indian] large, thin, crisp griddle-fried pancake or crepe, made with a fermented rice and lentil batter, sometimes topped with a spicy sauce and folded over. Usually served with sambar and chutney. *plural* **dosai, dosas**

doubles [Caribbean] a sandwich consisting of curried chickpeas (channa) placed between two small fried flatbreads, from Trinidad.

double cooked *see* **twice-cooked**

double cooked pork [Chinese] pork that is first boiled, then stir-fried with vegetables.

dragon phoenix [Chinese] popular nomenclature for combination dish of General Tso's chicken served alongside shrimp and mixed vegetables in Hunan sauce.

drunken [Thai] refers to dishes flavored with fresh basil leaf. *also* **drunkard's**

drunken noodles [Thai] soft flat noodles, stir-fried with fresh basil leaves and (usually) meat or shrimp, vegetables, and chile peppers. Thai noodle dishes are commonly eaten using chop sticks. *also called* **pad kee mao**

duba wat /doo′-bah-wutt/ [Ethiopian] a spicy

chopped pumpkin or squash stew, from northern Ethiopia.

dugh *see* **doogh**

dulet /du'-let/ [Ethiopian] tripe dish made from chopped sheep's stomach and liver sauteed with onion, salt, and pepper.

dum /dum/ [Indian] steamed in a closed vessel.

dumplings [Jamaican] boiled or fried morsels of dense kneaded dough, made with flour and milk. *also* **dumplins**

duona [Lithuanian] rye bread, commonly sour dough.

dwen jang, doenjang /den-jahng/ [Korean] fermented soy bean paste, similar to miso.

E

edamame /eh-dah-mah-meh/ [Japanese] fresh green soybeans steamed in the pod, which may be eaten by grasping the pods by hand and squeezing the individual beans directly into your mouth. (Do not eat the pod.) Also used in salads.

egg drop soup [Chinese] traditional soup made by slowly pouring beaten eggs into boiling broth to produce a suspension of thin, thoroughly-cooked egg threads, garnished with scallions and mushrooms.

egg foo yung [Chinese] egg-based fried patties similar to firm omelets, containing chopped vegetables and soy sauce and covered with a thick, salty, light brown gravy.

egg rolls [Chinese] a mixture typically of bits of pork, shrimp, and chopped vegetables placed on a square egg-noodle wrapper oriented in a diamond shape, rolled up into a cylinder, sealed and deep fried.

egusi [African] melon seeds that are ground into paste and added to soups, stews, or sauces, imparting an oily texture and a slightly nutty flavor.

emerald shrimp [Chinese] shrimp with green vegetables.

empanada /em-pah-nah′-da/ [Spanish, Latin American] pastry flour turnover filled with richly-seasoned meat or vegetables, usually served hot. *similar to* **Jamaican pattie**

empanizado /em-pah-nee-zah′-do/ [Cuban, other] meat or seafood item coated with bread crumbs and usually fried.

empress chicken [Chinese] marinated chicken pieces prepared with ginger and cornstarch and stir-fried.

enchiladas [Mexican] stuffed tortillas filled with a mixture of chicken or beef, salsa, chili powder, shredded cheese, and sour cream, then baked.

en croute /ahn-croot/ [French] enclosed in a flaky pastry envelope or shell.

enjera *see* **injera**

eru /air′-oo/ [West African] Yoruba (Nigerian) word for edible forest vine leaf, a popular nutritious vegetable.

escabeche 1. [Latin American] serving of pickled vegetables, especially small peppers, carrots, garlic, and cauliflower, as a condiment. **2.** [Spanish] meat or small fish soaked in a cold spicy marinade to preserve the flesh for several days.

es campur /ess-chomm-poor/ [Indonesian] dessert made with crushed ice and a cocktail of tropical fruits, topped with condensed milk and syrup. *similar to* **ice kacang**

escargots /ess-kahr-go/ [French] cooked snails, typically served in the shell in a butter, parsley, and garlic sauce.

escoveitched, escoveiched [Jamaican (from Spanish "pickled")] fried fish served hot (or cold-steeped) in spiced vinegar sauce with onions and hot peppers.

espagnole [various] *see* **brown sauce** (2.)

etouffee, étouffé /ay-too-fay/ **1.** [Cajun (from French "smothered")] Usually a traditional shrimp or crawfish stew served with a rich, thick spicy brown sauce. **2.** [French] indicates an item slow-cooked in a pan with a tight fitting cover: braised.

F

fagioli /fah-jhol′-ee *or* fah-zool′/ [Italian] beans.

fajitas /fah-hee′-tas/ [Tex-Mex] marinated meat and vegetables, sautéed and often served sizzling or flaming at tableside, traditionally placed by the diner on one of several tortillas, rolled up and eaten.

falafel, felafel /fuh-lah′-ful *also* fah-lah-fell/ [Middle Eastern] balls or morsels of ground chick peas, fava beans, and spices, deep fried. *see also* **ta'amia**

farina [various] grain or vegetable flour.

farinha /fah-reen-ya/ [Brazilian, other] cassava flour.

farfalle [Italian] bow-tie pasta.

farofa /fah-raw´-fah/ [Brazilian] roasted cassava-meal, typically flavored with butter, garlic, bacon, or other ingredients. It may be sprinkled liberally onto other foods.

fasolia /fah-soy´-ah/ [Greek] beans. *also* **fassolia**

fatayer /fah-tie´-ya/ [Middle Eastern] small pie or turnover, with a spinach, meat, or other filling, typically baked or fried.

fattoush [Lebanese, Syrian] a salad consisting of tomatoes and cucumber mixed with pita croutons, scallions, parsley, lemon, and mint. *also* **fatoush, fattouch, fattoosh, fettoosh** *other spellings*

fava beans /fah´-vah *or* fay´-vah/ [various] medium to large brown beans resembling lima beans, with a mild flavor.

feijao /fay-jhow/ [Portuguese, Brazilian] beans.

feijoada /fay-jhwah´-dah/ [Brazilian] popular "soul food" stew made with black beans and smoked meats, typically served with rice, collard greens, and roasted cassava meal (farofa). Authentic versions may contain tripe or pork parts not normally included in U.S. recipes. *also called* **feijoada completa**

felafel *see* **falafel**

fesenjan /fess-un-john´/ [Persian, Middle Eastern] chicken, lamb, or duck stewed in pomegranate and walnut sauce. *also* **fesenjaan, fesenjon, fessanjan**

festival [Jamaican] fried stick-shaped dumplings made of cornmeal, flour, and sugar.

feta [Greek, other] popular salty curdled cheese with a crumbly texture, of ancient origin. Originally made from sheep's and goat's milk, with modern imitations made from cow's milk.
(Note: government food safety experts advise pregnant women, older adults, and those with compromised immune systems not to eat feta unless it is labeled as made with pasteurized milk or is thoroughly cooked to bubbling hot.)

fettoosh, fettoush *see* **fattoush**

fettuccine /feh-tuh-chee´-nee/ [Italian] flat, ribbon-shaped noodles, narrower than Scotch tape. *common misspellings* **fettucini, fettucine**

fettuccine Alfredo /feh-tuh-chee´-nee al-fray´-doe/ [Italian] pasta noodles in thick cheese-cream sauce, sometimes made with raw egg.
(Note: foods prepared with raw [i.e., uncooked or unpasteurized] eggs may be unsafe for pregnant women, young children, older adults, and those with compromised immune systems.)

feuille de manioc /fooy-duh-man-yock/ [Senegalese] *same as* **cassava leaf**

filet mignon /fee-leh-meen-yohn/ [French] boneless beef tenderloin, considered one of the finest cuts of meat, sometimes cut into thick cylindrical steaks.

filezinho /feel-eh-zeen´-yo/ [Brazilian] beef tenderloin.

filo *or* **filo dough** *also* **phyllo** [Greek, other] a flaky pastry dough made of multiple paper-thin layers.

fines herbes /feen-zairb/ [French] popular mixture of very tender spring herbs, such as chopped parsley, tarragon, chervil, and chives.

firfir /fur-fur/ [Ethiopian] pieces of dried injera (sponge bread) mixed with meat, eggs, or vegetable stew, served hot, sometimes for breakfast.

firin sutlac /f-ruhn-soo(t)-lotch/ [Turkish] popular baked rice pudding dessert. *also* **firin sütlaç**

fish Veracruz *see* **pescado Veracruzana**

fitfit /f't-f't/ [Ethiopian] pieces of injera (sponge bread) mixed with meat or vegetable stew or salad, served cold.

five-spice [Chinese] a mixture of powdered spices consisting of fennel, cloves, cinnamon, star anise and anise, and sometimes Szechuan pepper, used in sauces or marinades.

flambé /flahm-bay/ [French] indicates an item doused with liquor and ignited for several seconds, typically presented tableside.

flan /flahn/ [Spanish, other] **1.** a sweet yellow dessert custard, often coated with a caramel layer. **2.** a small pastry shell filled with custard.

flautas /flout'-us/ [Mexican ("flutes")] rolled up tortillas filled with meat or chicken, then deep fried.

Florentine [U.S., other], **à la Florentine** [French] indicates an item made with spinach.

flour tortilla [northern Mexico, Tex-Mex] a soft tortilla made from wheat flour and shortening.

focaccia /fo-kot'-chee-uh/ [Italian] a firm flatbread commonly prepared with light, pungent toppings, resembling a dry pizza.

foie gras /fwah-grah/ [French] the enlarged liver of a force-fed goose or duck, as a delicacy.

food [Jamaican] ground provisions (plantains, yams, or bananas).

foo-foo *see* **fufu**

fool /fool/ [Arabic] **1.** a small, brown variety of fava beans popular in Middle Eastern recipes. **2.** fool beans served as a side dish. *also* **ful, foule, foul**

fool medames, fool mudammas *see* **ful medames**

foo yung *see* **egg foo yung**

forno, al forno [Italian] roasted in the oven.

fou-fou, foutou *see* **fufu**

foul, foule *see* **fool**

four seasons [Chinese] chicken, pork, shrimp, and beef with mixed vegetables.

Fra Diavolo /frah-dee-ah′-vo-lo/ [Italian (named after a legendary historical character)] a sauce combining seafood, tomato, garlic, hot peppers, and other ingredients, served over linguine or other pasta. *also* **Fra Diavlo**

frango a passarinho /frang′-go-(ah)-pah-sah-reen′-yo/ [Brazilian] crisp-fried marinated chicken pieces on the bone, with garlic.

freddi, freddo [Italian] cold.

fresco *see* **queso fresco**

fricassee /frick′-uh-see *or* free-kah-say/ [French, other] **1.** a method of cutting up and sautéing a few simple ingredients tossed in butter, such as meat, seafood, or vegetables. **2.** variable term for a method of cutting up, preparing, and frying various foods.

fried dumplings [Chinese, Thai] crispy pan-fried or deep-fried dumplings made of a dough shell filled with ground meat or seafood and chopped vegetables, typically served with a sauce.

fried rice [Chinese] pre-cooked rice subsequently stir-fried with chopped vegetables, with bits of meat, egg, or other ingredients added in.

frijoles /free-ho′-less/ [Latin American] beans.

frittata [Italian] omelet made with vegetables and cheese. Served hot as an entree or cold as an appetizer. *common misspelling* **fritatta**

fritter [various] a relatively shapeless blob of batter, usually fortified with chopped vegetable or fruit ingredients, which is submerged in hot oil and deep fried. May be served hot or cold depending on the recipe.

fritto misto /free′-toe-mee′-sto/ [Italian] bite-sized pieces of vegetables, meat, organ meats, or seafood dipped in batter and deep fried, served warm with lemon wedges.

fry bread [Native American] popular wheat dough flatbread deep fried in lard or vegetable oil and served hot.

fufu /foo-foo/ [African] a firm dumpling made from one of several starch-bearing vegetable products, such as fermented pounded yams, cassava, or plantains. *also* **foo-foo, fou-fou, foutou** /foo-too/

fugu [Japanese] raw blowfish, a relatively rare, expensive delicacy, prepared by specially licensed chefs, due to its poisonous parts.
(*Note: according to government food safety experts, pregnant women, young children, older adults, and those with compromised immune systems should avoid raw fish and seafood.*)

ful *see* **fool**

ful medames /full-muh-dom′-us/ [Egyptian, other] a classic stew or salad of fool (small fava beans) and lentils lightly simmered in oil or ghee with garlic, pepper, onion, parsley, and lemon or lime juice. May include chopped tomatoes, egg, or sausage. *also* **fool mudammas** *many other spellings*

funghi /foon'-ghee (hard "g")/ [Italian] mushrooms.

fusili /foo-zeel'-ee/ [Italian] long pasta twisted into a spiral shape.

fu yung, fu young [Chinese] scrambled egg patties flavored with soy sauce. *see* **egg foo yung**

G

ga /gaah/ [Vietnamese] chicken.

gado-gado /gah'-doe-gah'-doe/ [Indonesian] popular mixture of raw and lightly-cooked chopped vegetables (such as cabbage, carrots, spinach, and bean sprouts), chopped hard-boiled eggs, and tofu or tempeh, topped with a peanut sauce and shrimp-flavored chips. May be prepared mild or spicy.

gaeng /gang/ [Thai] curry. *see* **kaeng**

gaeng daeng /gang-dang/ [Thai] red curry. *see* **gaeng ped, red curry** *also* **kaeng daeng**

gaeng khiao wan /gang-kyaw-wahn/ [Thai ("hot sweet curry")] a hot curry made using fresh green chiles. *see* **green curry**

gaeng Masaman *see* **Massaman curry**

gaeng ped /gang ped/ [Thai] a dish prepared with a hot spicy curry sauce, usually implying red curry. *see* **red curry** *also* **kaeng phet, gaeng phed**

gaeng-phed ped-yang *see* **kang-ped bhet-yang**

gai, ghai /guy/ [Chinese, Thai] chicken.

gai kew /guy-Q/ [Chinese] large pieces of chicken breast, baked or stir-fried.

gai pad khing /guy pod king/ [Thai] sliced chicken stir-fried with ginger, onions, and mushrooms. Variably spicy.

gai pad med ma-muang /guy pod med mah-mwoong/ [Thai] stir-fried chicken with cashew nuts, typically with onions and various peppers.

gai tom kha *see* **tom kha gai.**

gajar halwa [Pakistani] carrot-flavored sweet dessert block.

gajrella [Pakistani] carrot-flavored **burfi.**

galaktoboureko /gah-lock-toe-boo′-ray-ko/ [Greek] baked custard pie covered with syrup.

galangal, galanga /guh-lahng′-gle/ [Thai] an aromatic vegetable in the ginger family with a unique flavor, commonly grated, popular for flavoring in Southeast Asian soups and dishes. *also called* **laos**

galbi *see* **kalbi**

gallo pinto /guy-oh-peen-toh/ [Costa Rican] cooked rice and cooked black beans sautéed with onions and served with mild sauce.

gambas /gahm-bahss/ [Spanish] shrimp.

gambas al ajillo /gahm′-bahss-ahl-ah-he′-yo/ [Spanish] shrimp in garlic sauce.

gamberi /gahm-beh-ree/ [Italian] shrimp.

gang /gang/ [Thai] curry. *see* **kaeng, gaeng**

garam masala /gah-rehm′ mah-sah′-lah/ [Indian] a fragrant, customized mixture of roasted, ground spices, commonly added near the end of the cooking process to enhance the aroma of foods. Typically includes cloves, cinnamon, cardamom, cumin, coriander, ginger, black pepper, and other spices in widely-varying proportions.

garbanzos [various] chick peas.

garden rolls *see* **goi cuon**

gari /gah'-ree/ **1.** [West African] grated or coarsely granulated cassava meal, slightly fermented, cooked in water or dry-fried, commonly combined with other ingredients in a manner similar to rice and consumed as a staple food for breakfast or lunch in Ghana. **2.** [Japanese] a term for pickled ginger.

garlic naan [Indian] baked flatbread made with garlic and herbs and cooked in a tandoor (clay oven).

garlic sauce [Chinese] a sweet, sometimes spicy mixture of minced garlic, soy sauce, vegetable oil, sugar, vinegar, and seasonings, sometimes with meat broth.

gazpacho /guh-spot'-show/ [Spanish] mildly-spiced pureed tomato-vegetable soup, served cold. Regionally variable.

gefilte fish /guh-fill'-tuh/ [Jewish ("stuffed")] molded balls or small cakes of ground fish, vegetables, egg, and matzo meal cooked in broth and served cold with horseradish.

gelato /jeh-lah'-toh/ [Italian] ice cream. *plural* **gelati** /jeh-lah'-tee/

General Tso's chicken *also* **General Tsao's chicken** /Tso's is pronounced "sows" (as in female hogs) or "djoz"/ [Chinese] popular Hunan dish of marinated chicken breaded and fried with garlic and ginger in a sweet, tangy sauce. In China, known as "ancestor meeting-place chicken" and arbitrarily re-named after a nine-teenth-century Chinese civil war general by a New York chef in the 1970's.

geoduck [U.S.] large clam native to the Pacific Northwest, primarily exported to Asia.

geow /gyow/ [Thai] won ton. *also* **keow, keaw**

ghai *see* **gai**

ghee /ghee (with a hard "g")/ [Indian] **1.** clarified butter, cooked and dehydrated, used as a cooking oil. **2.** (occasionally) vegetable shortening.

ghobi *see* **gobi**

ginataan /ghee-nah′-tah-ahn′/ [Filipino (from *ghata* "milky")] salty vegetable soup made with mung beans, onions, coconut milk, fish, and salty fermented fish paste. *also* **guinataan, ginataan**

ginger chicken [Chinese] variably prepared (baked, boiled, or stir-fried) chicken with ginger and other ingredients.

glass noodles *see* **bean thread, cellophane noodles**

gnocchi /nyuk′-ee/ [Italian ("lumps")] **1.** small potato and flour dumplings, either plain or flavored with cheese or other ingredients, usually boiled and served like pasta. **2.** similar little dumplings made without potatoes.

Goan /go on/ [Indian] Portuguese-influenced cooking style of Goa, a state on the west coast of India, known for a prevalence of vinegar marinades, coconut, cashews, very hot vindaloo and xacutti style dishes, and occasional pork dishes. *also* **Goanese**

gobi *also* **ghobi** /go′-bee/ [Indian] **1.** cauliflower, *also called* **phool gobi. 2.** occasionally, cabbage or kohlrabi.

gochujang *see* **kochujang**

goi cuon /gwy-koohn/ [Vietnamese] a popular fresh appetizer consisting of a transparent rice-noodle envelope wrapped around a filling of shrimp, lettuce, tiny rice noodles, and pork paté, all rolled up into a cylinder about the size of a thumb and served at room temperature with sweet peanut-soy dipping sauce. Usually grasped by hand, dipped, and eaten like miniature sandwiches. *also called* **summer rolls, salad rolls** (Note: sometimes called by misleading name of "fresh spring rolls" or "cold spring rolls," which may get confused with *cha gio*, the common Vietnamese crispy spring roll.)

golab jamun *see* **gulab jamun**

golubki /gah-wump-kee/ [Polish] stuffed cabbage rolls. *see also* **golubtsy, holubtsi**

golubtsy /go-lub′-tsee/ [Russian] cabbage leaf rolls stuffed with a mixture of ground meat and rice (or with onion, buckwheat, and rice) commonly served with tomato sauce or sour cream. *see* **holubtsi**

golveda /gol′-veh-dah/ [Nepalese] tomato. *also* **golbheda**

golveda ko achar [Nepalese] a chutney made with tomatoes, garlic, and cilantro.

gomen /go′-men/ [Ethiopian] collard greens, chopped and cooked with garlic and oil, served as a side dish.

gomen wat /go′-men-wutt/ [Ethiopian] collard greens stewed with onion, peppers, ginger, garlic, and hot spices.

gook, guk /gook/ [Korean] a broth-like soup to which rice is commonly added.

goong [Thai] shrimp. *also* **gung, kung, koong**

goong karee /goong-kah-ree/ [Thai] stir-fried shrimp with yellow curry sauce.

goong pad khing [Thai] stir-fried shrimp with ginger, black mushrooms, and spices.

goong pad med ma-muang [Thai] stir-fried shrimp and cashew nuts, with onion and bell pepper.

goong tod [Thai] seasoned deep-fried shrimp.

gorditas /gore-dee'-tuss/ [Latin American] **1.** thick tortillas, sometimes made with lard. **2.** small fried round corn patty with meat filling.

gored gored /gor'-ed-gor'-ed/ [Ethiopian] fine raw beef cut into bite-sized pieces, served warm mixed with butter and hot spices.
(*Note: foods prepared with raw meat may be unsafe for pregnant women, young children, older adults, and those with compromised immune systems.*)

goreng /go-rheng'/ [Indonesian] stir-fried.

gormeh sabzi /gore-may-sob-zee/ [Persian ("stew with vegetables")] popular rich stew with meat cubes, cilantro, spinach, parsley, chives, beans, fenugreek, and other ingredients.

gosh-e-feel *see* **goush-e-feel**

gosht /go-sht/ [Indian, Afghan] red meat.

goulash *see* **Hungarian goulash, gulasch**

gousfand /goose-fond/ [Afghan] a lamb. **gousfand gosht:** lamb meat.

goush-e-feel /goo-she-feel/ [Afghan ("elephant's ear")] a fried dessert pastry formed by pinching a flattened circle of dough together on one side, hence shaped like an elephant's ear, with pistachios and cardamom.

gousht /goo-sht/ [Persian] meat.

gram flour [Indian] lentil or chick pea flour. *also called* **besan**

grappa [Italian] a distilled alcoholic beverage made from the leftover skins, stems, and leaves of grapes after they have been pressed for wine making.

gra prow, grapao /krah-pow/ [Thai] sweet Thai basil leaf. *see* **kra prow**

grass jelly [Southeast Asian] a product made by cooling a tea of herbs or fruit to a soft jelly-like consistency and then cutting it into small cubes. Added to desserts.

gratiem /grah-tyem/ [Thai] garlic. *also* **kratiem, gratiam, gra-tiem, katiem, ka-tiam**

gratiem prik Thai /grah-tyem-prig-tie/ [Thai] stir-fry with garlic and white pepper. *also* **kratiem prik Thai, gratiem prig tai**

gravlax [Scandanavian] pickled salmon. (*Note: according to government food safety experts, pregnant women, young children, older adults, and those with compromised immune systems should avoid uncooked fish.*)

Greek salad [Greek] fresh salad with lettuce, olives, olive oil, vinegar, pepperoncini (slightly hot peppers), and feta cheese. (*Note: government food safety experts advise pregnant women, older adults, and those with compromised immune systems not to eat feta unless it is labeled as made with pasteurized milk.*)

green curry [Thai] dishes prepared with a very hot, sweet blend of ground spices and herbs, featuring fresh green chile peppers and typically including coriander, garlic, shallots, lemongrass, galangal, cumin, lime, salt, shrimp paste, or other ingredients. *also called* **kaeng khiao wan**

green tea [Asian] traditional popular beverage made by steeping relatively fresh, uncured tea leaves in hot (not boiling) water. Contains substances reputed to be beneficial for health.

grits [Southern] coarsely ground hominy, typically mixed with melted butter and served warm as a breakfast item.

groats /grotes/ whole kernels or large fragments of grains, such as buckwheat or oats.

groundnut stew [West African] a popular, variably-spicy stew commonly made with shredded chicken, peanut butter, sweet potatoes, onions, garlic, tomatoes, okra, and other ingredients. *also called* **peanut stew**

guacamole /gwah-kah-mo'-lay/ [Mexican (from Nahuatl, "avocado mixture")] avocado mixture or puree combined with salsa and lemon or lime juice, used as a dip, condiment, or an ingredient in other dishes.

guanabana [various] a large tropical fruit with an aromatic, juicy, whitish fibrous flesh, used to flavor ice cream and other dishes. A relative of the custard apple (sweetsop). *also called* **soursop**

guey teow, guay tiew /gway-dyow/ [Thai] fried flat rice noodles, commonly eaten using chop sticks. *see also* **kway teow**

gui [Korean] grill or grilled.

guinataan *see* **ginataan**

Gujarati [Indian] foods of the Gujarat state on the west coast of India, characterized by a prevalence of sweet-and-sour sauces, vegetarian dishes, and snacks.

guk *see* **gook**

gulab jamun /goo-lob´-jah-moon´/ [Indian] deliciously flavored deep-fried milk dough ball drenched with fragrant honey syrup, served warm as a dessert.

Gulasch /goo´-lush/ [German] a popular stew of beef or veal and vegetables seasoned with paprika. *see also* **Hungarian goulash**

gumbo [Southern U.S. especially Cajun/Creole (from West African *gom bo* "okra")] a variable, spicy slow-cooked stew or soup, made with meat or seafood, okra, and various other vegetables including onion, celery, tomatoes, and peppers. Traditionally served over rice.

gung *see* **goong**

gway teow [Malaysian] rice noodles, either ribbon shaped or in variously cut flat sheets. *see* **kway teow**

gyro *also* **gyro sandwich** /yee´-ro, jee´-ro/ [Greek] roasted ground meat shavings (usually lamb). The meat is generally cut from a large seasoned "meat loaf," which has been roasted on a rotating vertical spit, and served with grilled chopped vegetables, usually in a rolled-up pita or flatbread with a cucumber-yogurt dressing called **tzatziki.**

gyro salad [Greek, other] gyro meat and vegetable ingredients combined without the bread.

H

habanero peppers /hah-bah-neh'-ro/ [Mexican] extremely hot chile pepper, varying from green to red. *also called* **habanero chiles**

haggis /hag'-iss/ [Scottish] a sausage made from sheep stomach stuffed with organ meat and oat filling, boiled for more than four hours.

hakoo [Newar] black.

haldi [Indian] turmeric.

hallah *see* **challah**

hallal, halal [Arabic, other] foods conforming to Islamic dietary restrictions. Sacred.

halo-halo /hollow hollow/ [Filipino ("mix-mix")] popular dessert made with shredded ice, mixed fruit pieces, cooked beans, coconut milk, and sugar, typically served in a tall glass container and topped with ice cream or flan.

halupki *see* **holubtsi**

halva 1. [Middle Eastern, other] a confection of semolina flour or ground sesame, sweetened and flavored with other fruit or vegetable constituents and pressed into blocks. **2.** [Indian] similar product but made with lentils. *also* **halwa, helva, halvah**

hamantaschen /homm'-un-tosh'-un/ [Jewish] traditional triangular cookie or pastry with a sweet filling, associated with the Purim festivities. Typical fillings are a honey-poppy seed mixture, prunes, or other fruits.

happy family [Chinese] typically pork, beef, chicken, shrimp, and scallops or lobster, stir-fried with mixed vegetables.

har [Chinese] shrimp.

harira, harrira [Moroccan] a hearty soup traditionally served during Ramadan. Variable recipe includes chickpeas, onion, tomato, spices, and flour plus assorted other ingredients, such as coriander, parsley, celery, lentils, beans, or lamb. The soup is stirred continuously over low heat to achieve its customary thick texture.

harisa [North Africa] traditional hot red chile paste with garlic, coriander, caraway, cumin, olive oil, and salt. *also* **harrisa, harissa.**

haroset /hghah-ro-set/ [Jewish] a mixture of spiced chopped apples and nuts flavored with wine and cinnamon, traditionally used in the Passover ceremony.

har kew [Chinese] fried jumbo shrimp, typically with mushrooms and mixed vegetables.

harusame /hah-roo-sah-meh/ [Japanese] transparent noodles made from beans, rice, or potato. *see* **cellophane noodles**

Hasenpfeffer /hah′-zen-feff-er/ [German] marinated rabbit stew, variably seasoned.

haupia [Hawaiian] coconut pudding.

helva *see* **halva**

herbes de Provence /airb-duh-pro-vaunce/ [French (from *Provence* region in southeast France)] a mixture of herbs from the semi-arid region of Provence, typically including thyme, marjoram, savory, and sometimes rosemary, bay leaf, lavender, or sage.

Heringsalat /hair′-ing-sah-laht′/ [German] sweet or salty salad made with pickled herring and apples or onions, vinegar, cream, or other ingredients.

(*Note: according to government food safety experts, pregnant women, young children, older adults, and those with compromised immune systems should avoid uncooked fish.*)

hijiki, hiziki [Japanese] select seaweed leaves, steamed and dried, reputedly high in minerals. Typically used as an amendment to soups and salads.

hing [Indian] a spice containing a resin similar to garlic and onions. *also called* **asafoetida**

hocks (ham hocks) ankle joints of a hog, slow cooked or used to flavor soups.

ho fun *see* **hor fun**

hoi obb *also* **hoi oab** /hoy-obb/ [Thai] steamed mussels.

hoisin sauce /hoy-sin/ [Chinese] a sweet and spicy sauce made from ground fermented soybeans, sugar, garlic, and spices, used in cooking or as a condiment. *also* **hoi-sin, hoyshin**

hoja /ho'-hah/ [Latin American ("leaf")] a banana or plantain leaf wrapped around a food item for baking or steaming. Some recipes will substitute corn husks.

Hokkein noodles [Chinese, Thai, Malaysian] thin wheat noodles, named after an ethnic group in China and Singapore.

Hollandaise /uh-lawn-dez/ [French] a creamy, lightly cooked sauce made with butter, egg yolk, and lemon.
(*Note: foods prepared with lightly cooked eggs may be unsafe for pregnant women, young children, older adults, and those with compromised immune systems.*)

holubtsi /huh-loob'-chee/ [Ukrainian, other] stuffed cabbage leaves filled with ground meat and rice, or with kasha, covered with tomato sauce and baked. *also* **halupki, holupki** *see* *also* **golubtsy**

hominy [Native American, other] corn kernels with the outer casing removed.

hommus *see* **hummus**

hom pah [Thai] shrimp wrapped in a wonton wrapper and fried.

honey sesame chicken [Chinese] baked skinless chicken pieces with sesame and mustard coating, served with honey-flavored dipping sauce.

hoppin' John [Southern] black-eyed peas and rice flavored with ham or bacon, sometimes seasoned with hot peppers.

horchata /or-chah´-tah/ **1.** [Spanish, Latin American] a popular sweetened, milk-like beverage, called *horchata de chufa*, made from an aromatic Egyptian tuber, flavored with cinnamon, and served cool. **2.** a beverage similar to horchata de chufa, made from rice, nuts, or seeds. *also* **orchata**

hor fun /hor-foon/ [Malaysian, Chinese] broad thick rice noodles, cut into strips and fried in a wok. *also* **ho fun**

horiatiki /hor-ya´-tee-kee/ [Greek ("rural village style")] a traditional tossed salad made with tomato wedges, chunks of cucumber, green peppers, feta cheese, sliced onions, olives, olive oil, oregano, and salt, with no lettuce.
(Note: government food safety experts advise pregnant women, older adults, and those with compromised immune systems not to eat feta unless it is labeled as made with pasteurized milk.)

hors d'oeuvres /or-dervz/ [French] small appetizers.

hot and sour soup [Chinese] a soup made with thin pieces of vegetables or meats, hot pepper, and vinegar.

hot pot [Mongolian, Chinese] a method of preparing food in which the diner places small or thin pieces of vegetables, seafood, meats, or organ meats into a vessel of boiling broth at the table, cooks them to the desired degree, then removes them from the broth using chopsticks, a fondue fork, or a wire strainer. The freshly cooked items are then dipped into a sauce and eaten.

hrin /hghrin/ [Jewish, Russian, Ukrainian, other] a kind of relish made with beets, horseradish, and sugar, traditional during Easter and Passover. *also* **chrin, hryn**

huevos rancheros /way'-vose-ran-chair'-ose/ [Mexican] baked or fried eggs and salsa served with crisp fried tortillas.

hummus /hum'-us/ [Middle Eastern (from Arabic "chick pea")] popular dip made with pureed chickpeas, ground sesame, garlic, lemon juice, and salt. Typically served as an appetizer dip with pita bread wedges. *also* **hummous, hommus**

Hunan, Hunan-style [Chinese] regional cooking style of the river, lake, and mountainous areas of Hunan province, characterized by an elaborate variety of ingredients and cooking methods, including relatively colorful and varied vegetable constituents, meats, smoked meats and fish, the use of fresh hot chile peppers, black bean sauce, and sophisticated seasoning and marinating. Dishes are commonly steamed, simmered, and stewed, as well as fried.

Hunan bean curd [Chinese] tofu cubes cooked with meat and hot spicy black bean sauce.

Hunan chicken [Chinese] marinated chicken pieces stir-fried in ginger, garlic, and hot pepper sauce.

Hunan pork [Chinese] marinated shredded pork cooked in a hot, spicy wine, soy, and vinegar sauce.

Hunan shrimp [Chinese] shrimp cooked with hot spicy black bean sauce.

Hungarian goulash /goo′-losh/ [Hungarian] a slow-cooked stew of beef, onions, garlic, and other vegetables, with paprika, black pepper, and other seasonings.

hunkar begendi /hoon′-kahr-bay′-en-dee/ [Turkish ("sultan's delight")] popular dish made from the interior of roasted eggplants, which are mashed and re-cooked with milk, cheese, and spices.

hwe, hwae /hweh/ [Korean] raw.
(*Note: according to government food safety experts, pregnant women, young children, older adults, and those with compromised immune systems should avoid raw fish and seafood.*)

I

iab /ah-eeb′/ [Ethiopian] cottage cheese, sometimes flavored with yogurt and seasonings. *also* **ayib, iyb**

ice kacang /ice keh-chong′/ [Malaysian] a popular dessert made with shredded ice (similar to a "snow cone") variably topped with red beans, corn, palm seeds, grass jelly, coconut milk or condensed milk, and syrup. *also* **ais kacang** *see also* **halo-halo**

idli /id'-lee/ [South Indian] steamed fermented-rice dumplings, molded into tapered patties ("flying saucer" shaped). Generally served with sambar and chutney. *also* **idly, iddly**

ikan /ee-kahn/ [Indonesian, Malaysian] fish.

imam bayildi /ee-mom-buy-ill-dee/ [Turkish ("the Imam fainted")] stuffed eggplants split lengthwise and filled with a mixture of eggplant, tomatoes, onions, garlic, and seasonings, then baked. A famous dish.

imperial rolls *see* **cha gio, spring rolls**

Imperial soup [Chinese] soup made with minced chicken, seafood, vegetables, and egg white.

incik /in-cheek/ [Turkish] lamb shank.

indugghia /een-doo'-ghee-ah (hard g)/ [Italian] an organ meat sausage, a predecessor of **andouille.**

injera /in-jair-ah/ [Ethiopian] a large, soft, very flat elastic sponge bread with a slightly sour flavor, made from **tef** flour (or sometimes substitute grains). It is torn into small pieces to grasp individual mouthfuls of stewed dishes (ideally using the right hand). It also is used as an edible platter onto which foods are served, family-style, in an Ethiopian restaurant. *also* **ingera, enjera, njera**

insalata /in-sah-lah-tah/ [Italian] salad.

Irish moss [various] carrageen, a type of seaweed that is dried and ground, commonly added to milk and sugar to make a shake-type beverage or pudding.

Iskender kebab /ees-ken-der-kah-bob/ [Turkish, named after the originator] doner kebab (shaved meat) served over sautéed pita bread drenched in yogurt, with tomato sauce and meat broth.

iyb *see* **iab**

J

jackfruit [Indian, other] a gigantic tropical fruit related to the fig and breadfruit, with a sometimes foul odor, a sweet, fragrant interior, and a meaty texture.

Jaegerschnitzel /yay-gur-shnit-sul/ [German ("hunter's cutlets")] pork or veal, sliced or pounded flat, topped with a creamy mushroom sauce. *also* **Jägerschnitzel**

jaggery [various] unrefined palm sugar.

jalapeño pepper /hah-lah pain'-yo/ [various] a hot green pepper about two inches long.

jalfrezi, jalfrazi [Indian] spicy stir-fry dish, typically with onions, tomatoes, and bell peppers.

Jamaican pattie *see* **pattie**

jambalaya /johm-buh-lie'-uh/ [Cajun/Creole] popular spicy seasoned stew or casserole including meat, poultry, seafood, andouille sausage, vegetables, and herbs in a tomato-based sauce, traditionally served over rice.

Jânis' /yah-niss/ [Latvian] a popular soft cheese flavored with caraway seeds, commonly spread on bread for breakfast. Particularly associated with the celebration of the summer solstice. *also* **Janis cheese, Janu siers**

jap chae, japchae *see* **chop chae**

jasmine tea [various] fragrant hot beverage made from tea leaves flavored with jasmine flowers.

jeera [Indian] cumin.

jerk [Jamaican, West Indian] a popular seasoning mixture including allspice, scallions, garlic, Scotch bonnet peppers, salt, black pepper, vinegar, and other ingredients.

jerk chicken [Jamaican, West Indian] marinated smoked chicken prepared with Jerk seasoning, traditionally cooked over a pimiento wood fire.

jerky [various] seasoned dried beef strips.
(*Note: jerky that is not commercially prepared in the U.S. may be unsafe for pregnant women, young children, older adults, and those with compromised immune systems.*)

jicama /hee'-kah-mah/ [Mexican, other] large, firm root vegetable, which is peeled and shredded or slivered, then added to salads, boiled, or roasted. It is sometimes served as a side dish or as an appetizer with lemon juice sprinkled on it.

jigae *see* **chigae**

jingha [Indian] prawns or shrimp.

jjigae *see* **chigae**

jollof rice /jaw'-luff *or* joe'-luff/ [West African] rice prepared with tomatoes, peppers, onions, and seasonings, usually served with meat or fish.
also **jolof rice, djolof rice**

jugos /hoo'-gose/ [Spanish] juice.

julienne /joo-lee-en'/ [various] to cut into thin slivers.

jus de bissap *see* **bissap juice**

K

ka *see* **kha, galangal**

kabab /kuh-bob'/ **1.** [various] morsels of meat or vegetables, usually marinated, then assembled on a skewer and grilled, or (uncommonly) deep fried. **2.** [Persian] meat or fowl. *also* **kabob, kebab**

kabab-e barg [Persian] pieces of fine meat fillets, which are flattened and marinated, skewered and roasted, served with rice and sumac powder.

kabab-e kubideh *see* **kubideh kabob**

kachori /kah-chore'-ee/ [Indian] a deep-fried circle of rich, puffed-up pastry dough filled with spiced vegetable, lentil, or fruit mixtures, served as an appetizer or side dish. *also* **kachauri**

kadayif /kah-dah-eef/ [Turkish] *see* **kataifi**

kadhai *see* **karahi**

kadhi *see* **karhi**

kadu /kah-doo/ [Afghan] sautéed or stewed pumpkin, as a side dish.

kae /kye/ [Ethiopian ("red")] indicates an item cooked with berbere (hot red pepper seasoning). *also* **key, keye, kay, kaye**

kae atar wat /kye-ah-tar-watt/ [Ethiopian] spicy stew of green or yellow split peas and red pepper seasoning.

kae mesir wat /kye-mess'r-watt/ [Ethiopian] spicy stew of red or brown lentils cooked with berbere (hot pepper seasoning).

kaeng /gang/ [Thai] curry. *also* **kang, gaeng, gang**

kaeng daeng /gang dang/ [Thai] *see* **red curry**

kaeng ka-ri [Thai] *see* **yellow curry**

kaeng khiao wan /gang-kyaw-wahn/ [Thai ("hot sweet curry")] hot curry made from fresh green chiles. *also* **gaeng khiao wan** *see* **green curry**

kaeng ped *see* **kaeng phet**

kaeng phet, kang ped /gang ped/ [Thai] a dish prepared with a hot spicy curry sauce, usually implying red curry. *see* **red curry**

kaeng-phet pet-yang /gang ped bet-yaang/ [Thai] roast duck with red curry. (*innumerable other spellings*)

kafta *see* **kofta**

kai /guy/ [Thai] chicken.

kai pad med ma-muang /guy-pot-met-mah-mwong/ [Thai] stir-fried chicken with cashew nuts, typically with onions and various peppers.

kalamari *see* **calamari**

kalbi [Korean] popular dish consisting of beef short ribs long-marinated in Korean barbecue sauce, often cooked on a grill at the table, typically served "ssam" style (to be rolled up by the diner in a lettuce leaf, along with various vegetables and sauce, and eaten). *also* **kal bi, galbi**

kallaloo *see* **calalu**

kalonji, kalongi [Indian] a spice, also called nigella, made from black seeds of a type of onion, traditionally used for pickling or for adding a nutty flavor to naan.

Kalua pig [Hawaiian] whole roast pig.

kana /kah-nah/ [Thai] the leafy greens of Chinese broccoli. *also* **khana, ka-na**

kang /gang/ [Thai] curry. *see* **kaeng**

kang-ped bhet-yang /gang-ped-bet-yaang/ [Thai] roast duck with red curry. (*innumerable other spellings*)

kao [Thai] rice. *see* **khao**

kaong [West African, Filipino] seeds from palms, which are pounded into butter or boiled.

kaprow, ka prao *see* **kra prow**

kapusta [Polish, Russian, Ukrainian, other] **1.** a cabbage dish similar to sauerkraut. **2.** cabbage.

karahi /kah-rye′ *also* kah-dhah′-hee/ [Pakistani, Indian] **1.** traditional bowl-shaped iron pan with two handles resembling a thick wok. **2.** a dish cooked in a karahi, typically with ghee, tomatoes, onions, bell peppers, and spices. *also* **kadhai, korai, karai**

karee [Thai] *see* **yellow curry**

karela /kar-eh-lah/ [Indian] bitter gourd.

karhi /kuh-ree/ [Indian] soft dumplings made from chickpea flour and chopped vegetables. Usually served in a sauce made with chickpea flour, yogurt or buttermilk, and various spice mixtures. *also* **kadhi**

kari /kah-ree/ **1.** [Indian] a culinary herb with a curry flavor, sometimes called curry leaf. **2.** [Malaysian, Indonesian] curry.

karkadeh [Egyptian] hibiscus beverage. *similar to* **bissap juice**

Kartoffelklösse /car-tof′-fel-klur-seh/ [German] dumplings made of potatoes, flour, eggs, and seasonings, often filled with croutons or prunes. *also* **Kartoffelkloesse**

Kartoffelpuffer [German] *see* **potato pancakes**

kasha /kah'-shuh/ [Russian, Jewish] **1.** cooked buckwheat groats. **2.** any cooked whole grain, such as buckwheat, barley, or oats.

kasha varnishkes /kah'-shuh var-nish'-kz/ [Jewish] buckwheat groats combined with bow-tie pasta, served hot.

kashk /koshk/ [Persian] whey.

kashk-e bademjan /koshk'-ee-bahd-em-john'/ [Persian] eggplant with a whey-yogurt dressing. *also* **kashk-o-bademjan**

Kashmiri /kosh-mee'-ree/ [Indian, Pakistani] a classic cuisine characterized by spiced meat dishes, the use of milk and yogurt, saffron, hing, and other delicate seasonings, and dried fruits and nuts.

Kashmiri naan /non/ [Indian] baked white-flour flatbread made with dried fruits and nuts. *see* **naan**

kasseri /kah-sehr'-ree/ [Greek] salty, pungent, semi-soft cheese commonly made with cow's or sheep's milk.

kastinis *or* **kastinys** [Lithuanian] butter-cream dip.

kataif /kah-tah-eef'/ [Middle Eastern, other] pastry made from wheat dough rolled into pancake-thin sheets, filled with cheese or nuts, covered with another layer of dough, oven baked, and topped with sugar syrup, usually served after sundown during Ramadan. *also* **qataif, kataifi, kadayif**

kataifi /kah-tah-ee'-fee/ [Middle Eastern, Greek] **1.** a type of shredded dough used to make pastries. **2.** a pastry similar to baklava, made with shredded dough.

katchalu [Afghan] potato.

kati [Thai] coconut.

katiem, ka-tiam *see* **kratiem.**

kawati *see* **kwati**

kay, kaye *see* **kae**

kazan dibi /kah′-zahn-deeb′-eh/ [Turkish ("left-over in the pot")] popular carmelized pudding dessert made with milk, sugar, cinnamon, and flavorings.

keaw nam [Thai] hot, spicy wonton soup with pork, mushrooms, scallions, and vegetables or seaweed. *see also* **geow**

kebab *see* **kabab**

kecap *see* **ketjap**

kedgeree /kitch-ree/ [English, adapted from Indian *khichri*] a dish of rice cooked with bits of fish and chopped hard-boiled eggs.

kedjenou [Cote d'Ivoire] chicken slow-cooked in a closed vessel with tomatoes, onion, garlic, and ginger.

keema [Indian] ground meat.

keema matar [Indian] curried ground meat cooked with green peas (and tomatoes).

keema naan [Indian] flatbread filled with mild spiced ground beef or lamb.

kee mao /kee-moww/ [Thai] *see* **drunken noodles.** *also* **kee mow, khee mao**

kefir /keh-fihr′/ [Caucasus region] fermented milk beverage, sometimes mildly alcoholic.

keftedes /kef-ted′-ess/ [Greek] meatball dish, similar to kofta.

kem [Thai] salty.

kenkey /keng-kay/ [West African] fermented corn dough mixture, formed into fist-sized balls with

97

a smooth, starchy texture and a sour flavor, cooked by steaming in a banana leaf or corn husk, popular in Ghana.

keow *see* **geow**

keow wan *see* **khiao wan, green curry**

ketjap *more correctly* **kecap** /ketchup/ [Indonesian] soy sauce.

ketjap manis [Indonesian] sweet soy sauce used for marinating or cooking, or as a condiment.

kew /cue/ [Chinese] large-sized chunks or pieces of an item, such as chicken, shrimp, or steak.

key, keye /kye/ [Ethiopian] the color red, indicating a dish cooked with berbere (hot red pepper seasoning). *see* **kae**

key wat /kye-watt/ [Ethiopian] small cubes of beef or lamb stewed with berbere (hot pepper seasoning). *also* **keywot, keye wat** *see also* **kae**

kha [Thai] galangal.

khai /kye/ [Thai] egg.

khaja [Nepalese] a collection of dishes popular during "tea breaks" (i.e., pauses in the workday) including rice, corn, and potato items.

khajoor /kah-juhr/ [Indian] dates.

khana *see* **kana**

khao, kao /cow/ [Thai] rice.

khao niao [Thai] a sticky, firm, high-protein rice, sometimes called "sweet rice," commonly used in desserts, or in northern Thailand as a staple food. *also* **khao niew, khao neow**

khao pad /cow pot/ [Thai] fried rice. *also* **khao phad, kao pad**

khee mao *see* **kee mao**

kheer [Indian] rice pudding, commonly made with nuts, raisins, and cardamom.

khiao wan /kyaw-wahn/ [Thai ("hot sweet")] *see* **green curry**. *also* **keow wan, khiew wah, khiaw waan**

khichri /kitch-ree/ [Indian] rice and lentils cooked together. *also* **khitchri, kichri, kitchree** *other spellings*

khing [Thai] ginger. *also* **king**

khitchri *see* **khichri**

khoresht, khoresh [Persian] any of a wide variety of dishes of cooked meat and vegetables or fruits, served in their juices as a stew-like sauce, typically with white rice.

khouzi [Arabian] stuffed whole lamb or young camel, baked or roasted.

kibbeh [Middle Eastern, other] popular dish made from finely chopped meat, bulgur wheat, and pine nuts, molded into various round or other shapes and typically fried or baked, sometimes served raw. *also* **kibbe, kibbi**
(*Note: foods prepared with raw meat may be unsafe for pregnant women, young children, older adults, and those with compromised immune systems.*)

kibe /kib-eh/ [Ethiopian] butter made from sour milk *see* **niter kebbeh.**

kichri, kichree *see* **khichri**

kielbasa /keel-bah′-sah/ [Polish, other] spicy sausage, often flavored with garlic.

kik /kick/ [Ethiopian] **1.** yellow split peas **2.** peas, lentils, or beans in a split rather than a whole state.

kik alicha /kick′-ah-letch′-uh/ [Ethiopian] split peas cooked with onions and mild spices.

kilkil /k′l-k′l/ [Ethiopian ("to boil")] beef, lamb, or vegetable mixture, such as a stew, cooked in a pot of water for a long time until the ingredients are tender.

kim chi [Korean, other] **1.** classic fermented cabbage preparation with salt, hot chiles, and up to twenty flavoring ingredients including garlic, shrimp paste, and ginger. **2.** other vegetables prepared kim chi style. *also* **kimchi, kim chee**

kinche /kin-cheh/ [Ethiopian] cracked wheat porridge with melted butter, a common breakfast meal, sometimes a lunch or dinner side dish.

king *see* **khing**

kinilaw /kee′-nee-lao/ [Filipino (from *kilaw* "raw")] raw tuna or other seafood prepared with tuba (palm-flower) vinegar, garlic, ginger, and hot peppers.
(*Note: according to government food safety experts, pregnant women, young children, older adults, and those with compromised immune systems should avoid raw fish and seafood.*)

kîsêlis /chee-sells/ [Latvian] traditional preparation of stewed fruits, for example prunes, apples, apricots, and grapes, made into a thick syrup or jelly and eaten with desserts. *also* **kiselis**

kishke /kish′-kuh/ [Jewish, other] **1.** variable recipe for a soft, smooth-textured sausage made with chicken fat, flour, and bread crumbs stuffed into beef intestine. Some versions include organ meats. **2.** baked vegetarian sausage loaf resembling traditional kishke. *also* **kishka, kiske, kiska** *also called* **stuffed derma**

kitchri, kitchree *see* **khichri**

kitfo /k't-foe/ [Ethiopian] spiced chopped raw beef, served warm. May be ordered raw (ti're kitfo), slightly cooked ("lub-lub" style), or even fully cooked (tibs kitfo) if requested.
(*Note: foods prepared with raw meat may be unsafe for pregnant women, young children, older adults, and those with compromised immune systems.*)

Klösse /klur'-seh *or* klah'-hghuh/ [German] dumplings. *also* **Kloesse**

Knackwurst /nock-voorsht/ [German] a cooked smoked pork and beef sausage with a strong garlic flavor, somewhat thicker and shorter than a hot dog. It may be boiled or grilled and is served hot, commonly with sauerkraut.

knaidel /k(uh)-nay'-dul/ [Jewish] matzoh ball. *plural* **knaidlach** /k(uh)-nade-lohkh/

knish /k(uh)-nish'/ [Jewish, other] fried or baked pastry with a seasoned mashed potato filling, consumed as an appetizer, snack, or side dish. Sometimes made with chopped liver or cheese.

Knockwurst *see* **Knackwurst**

knödel /kner'-dul/ [various] Central European dumplings made with pasta flour and other ingredients. *also* **knoedel**

koay teow [Malaysian] rice noodles. *see* **kway teow**

Kobe beef [Japanese] a special, expensive type of beef that is bred and fed to produce a quality of tenderness and flavor that is highly prized.

kochujang [Korean] hot red pepper paste. *also* **gochujang, kochu chang**

koeksister [South African] braided pastry, deep fried and soaked in syrup.

koening *see* **kuning**

kofta /kuhf-tah/ [Indian, many other] a ball-shaped croquet or dumpling of curried minced meat or mashed vegetables, grilled on a skewer, deep fried, or baked. For example, meatballs. *also* **köfte, kufta, koofta, koofteh, kufteh, kofte**

kofta kabob /kuhf-tah-kuh-bob/ [Indian, other] curried minced meatballs, skewered and cooked in a tandoor or deep fried.

kombu [Japanese] edible kelp (seaweed) processed as a cooked noodle or in other forms. *also* **konbu**

koobideh *see* **kubideh**

koong [Thai] shrimp.

korai *see* **karahi**

korma, kurma [Indian] **1.** popular meat curry traditionally prepared by braising in an oven, then cooking in a light-colored gravy made with yogurt, cream, or coconut milk and almonds or cashews, often mild but sometimes spicy. **2.** In Western adaptations, a dish with a mild, creamy sauce incorporating similar ingredients to the traditional korma,

kose, kosai /ko'-seh/ [Ghanaian] *see* **akara**

kosher [Jewish] conforming to religious dietary laws.

kosheri [Egyptian, Lebanese, other] rice topped with lentils and onions, and commonly pasta and tomato sauce. *also* **koshari, koshary**

kothay, kothey [Tibetan] fried dumplings, similar to pot stickers.

kra prow [Thai] sweet basil leaf. *also* **kra prao, krapao, gra prao, kaprow,** *other spellings*

kratiem /grah-tyem/ [Thai] garlic. *also* **gratiem,**

kra tiem, kratiam, katiem

kratiem prig Thai /grah-tyem-prig-tie/ [Thai] stir-fry with garlic and white pepper.

kreplach /krep'-lohkh/ [Jewish] triangular (or square) egg-noodle dumplings with a meat or cheese filling, resembling ravioli and floated in a soup like wontons.

krob /graub/ [Thai] crispy deep-fried item.

kuai tiao, kuay teow *see* **kway teow**

kubideh kabob [Persian] ground meat, typically lamb, beef, or veal, molded lengthwise on a skewer and grilled, then removed and served with bread or rice. *also* **kabab-e kubideh, koobideh kabob**

Kuchen /koo'-hghen/ [German ("cake")] generic term for cake made from flour, sugar, eggs, and fat.

kueh lapis *see* **kuih lapis**

kueh teow *see* **kway teow**

kufteh [Persian ("pounded")] meatballs. *see* **kofta**

kugel [Jewish, other] a baked casserole or pudding made of eggs, vegetables, noodles, fruits, nuts, or other ingredients, prepared as a side dish or as a dessert.

kugelis [Lithuanian] potato pudding flavored with onions and bacon.

kuih /kway/ [Malaysian] cake.

kuih ketayap /kway keh-tie'-epp/ [Malaysian] thin crepe made of rice flour, often flavored with pandan leaf and filled with a sweet filling, such as sugared coconut.

kuih lapis /kway lah-peace'/ [Malaysian] layered cake that has a firm, slightly greasy texture, made from coconut milk and rice flour. *also* **kueh lapis**

kulcha /kull'-cha/ [Indian] baked white-flour flatbread, which can be made plain or with onions and coriander or other vegetable ingredients, or with paneer.

kulfi, kulfee [Indian] molded ice cream with a fudge-like consistency, made with condensed milk and nuts.

kulich /koo-leach/ [Russian] a rich, sweet Easter bread baked in a tall mold and decorated with a rose.

kung [Thai] shrimp.

Kung Pao, Kung Po [Chinese] pieces of meat or tofu stir-fried with peanuts, mixed vegetables, and hot chile peppers in a sauce. Named after a character in a Szechuan legend.

kuning /koo-ning/ [Indonesian] yellow-colored dish made with turmeric and herbs. *also* **koening**

kurma *see* **korma**

kutia [Ukrainian] a sweetened mixture of boiled wheat kernels and ground poppyseeds topped with nuts, traditionally served on Christmas eve.

kvas /k-vahss/ [Russian] a popular fermented beverage made from variable ingredients, for example bread or beets. Sometimes used in soups. *also* **kvass**

kwati /kwah-tee/ [Newar] a hearty nine-bean soup popular in Nepal. *also* **quantee**

kway teow /kway-tyow/ [Malaysian, Thai] rice noodles, either ribbon-shaped or in variously cut flat sheets. *also* **koay teow, kueh teow, gway teow,** *other spellings*

L

laab *see* **larb**

laban [Middle Eastern] yogurt.

labneh [Middle Eastern] strained yogurt cheese stored in olive oil, typically made into a dip. *also* **labne, labaneh, labane, lebne,** *other spellings*

lad na *see* **lard na, rad na**

lahma bi ajeen /laham-(bh)-jheen'/ [Middle Eastern] Arabic flat yeast bread with tomato and meat toppings, somewhat similar to pizza. *also* **lahm bi ajeen** *contraction* **lahmajun, lamajun**

lahmacun /lah-mah-juhn/ [Turkish, Armenian] popular thin-crust "pizza" with meat topping. *also* **lahmajun, lamacun**

Lake Tung Ting shrimp [Chinese (after Lake Dongting in northern Hunan province)] shrimp and mixed vegetables with a cooked egg-white coating or sauce.

laksa /lock'-sah/ [Southeast Asian] a rich, creamy, aromatic coconut milk and rice-noodle soup made with tofu, shrimp, or fish, and hot chiles.

laksa Penang /lock'-sah-puh-nang'/ [Malaysian] aromatic laksa broth and noodles, normally made without coconut milk.

lamajun, lamacun *see* **lahmacun**

lamb karahi [Indian/Pakistani] lamb chunks, sometimes with tomatoes, onions, ginger, or bell peppers, with herbs and spices, cooked in a karahi (a wok-like cooking pan).

lamb rogan josh *see* **rogan josh**

laos [Southeast Asian] galangal. *also* **laos root, Laos ginger**

larb /lobb/ [Thai] a salad made from ground meat (most commonly chicken) with onion and lemon or lime juice. May contain semi-cooked, rare, or raw meat. *also* **laab**
(Note: foods prepared with raw meat may be unsafe for pregnant women, young children, older adults, and those with compromised immune systems.)

lard na, lad na /rodd-nah/ [Thai] stir-fried flat rice noodles, usually with a selected meat or tofu, broccoli (or Chinese broccoli), and a gravy sauce. *see also* **rad na**

lasagna /lah-zahn'-yuh/ [Italian, other] **1.** famous dish made from multiple alternating layers of pasta sheets, ground meat or vegetable, tomato sauce, and egg-cheese mixture. **2.** any pasta with a ruffled edge. *also* **lasagne**

lassi /lah'-see/ [Indian] refreshing yogurt beverage, sweet or salted or flavored with fruit, blended to the consistency of a light milkshake.

latkes /lot'-kz/ [Jewish, other] pancakes, traditionally made from potatoes and commonly served during Chanukah with applesauce and sour cream.

lavash, lavosh [Persian, Armenian, other] rather large, thin, unleavened flatbread, either soft or in the form of a cracker.

laulau [Hawaiian] pork butt and fish wrapped with spinach or other greens, steamed at length in a banana leaf or corn husk.

Lebkuchen /leb-koo-hghen/ [German] **1.** variable recipe for soft, chewy spiced cookies made with candied fruit and nuts, covered with a chocolate or sugar glaze. A special Christmas treat. **2.** a firm hard cookie used to make gingerbread houses.

leb-leb *see* **lub-lub**

lebneh, lebne *see* **labneh**

leche /ley'-cheh/ [Mexican, other] milk. *see also*
arroz con leche, tres leches

leche flan *see* **flan**

lechon /leh-chonn'/ [Filipino] whole roast suck-
ling pig, served as the centerpiece of a meal on
special occasions and holidays.

leek [various] a vegetable resembling a large green
onion, but with a milder, sweeter flavor.

lefse [Scandanavian] baked thin-rolled potato
bread patty resembling a tortilla.

lega tibs /leg-uh-t'bs/ [Ethiopian] cubes of tender marinated prime beef or lamb, lightly sautéed
with onions, green peppers, and other ingredients, variably seasoned.

lemon chicken [Chinese] fried or steamed marinated chicken with spices and fresh lemon juice.

lemon grass [Southesast Asian] the bulbous base
of a large stiff grass, which is chopped into fragments and used to impart a lemon-like flavor
and fragrance to soups and other dishes. *also*
lemongrass

linguine *also* **linguini** /ling-gwee'-nee/ [Italian]
flat pasta noodles less than one-quarter inch
wide.

Linzertorte /lin'-tser-tor-tuh/ [German, Austrian
(named after city of Linz)] a sweet baked fruit
tart covered by cross-hatched strips of pastry
dough, typically filled with raspberry preserves.

llapingacho /yah-ping-got'-cho/ [Ecuadorian]
popular Andean potato and cheese pancake or
molded pattie, sometimes accompanied by fried

sweet plantains or fried eggs.

lobster sauce [Chinese] a thickened sauce made from vegetable oil, ground pork, wine, chicken broth, cornstarch, egg and sugar, but no lobster.

lokum *see* **Turkish delight**

lo mein /lo-main/ [Chinese] wheat noodles similar to spaghetti.

lomi-lomi [Hawaiian ("to massage")] salted raw salmon salad with tomato and onion, mixed together by hand.
(*Note: according to government food safety experts, pregnant women, young children, older adults, and those with compromised immune systems should avoid raw fish and seafood.*)

lomo saltado [Peruvian] thin-sliced beef sautéed with hot peppers, onion, tomato, and other vegetables.

long bean [Chinese] an extremely long variety of string bean.

loobia [Persian] green beans.

loubia b'dersa [Algerian] loubia bil luz with chile peppers, garlic, and cumin.

loubia bil luz [Algerian, Middle Eastern] sautéed whole string beans with seasoning.

lover's shrimp [Chinese] shrimp prepared in two contrasting styles on the same plate, for example a hot red chile sauce and a light garlic wine sauce.

lox [Jewish] smoked or salt-cured raw salmon, often sliced thin and arranged on a platter. *see also* **gravlax**
(*Note: according to government food safety experts, pregnant women, young children, older adults, and those with compromised immune systems are advised not to eat smoked seafood such*

as lox unless it is contained in a cooked dish, such as a casserole.)

lub-lub, leb-leb /lebb-lebb/ [Ethiopian] finely chopped beef seasoned with hot peppers, cooked rare. *see* **kitfo**

lumpia /loohm'-pea-uh/ [Filipino] popular appetizer similar to a spring roll, with more emphasis on meats in the filling.

lung har /lung-hah/ [Chinese] lobster.

lung har kew [Chinese] large pieces of lobster, typically combined with mixed vegetables.

lychee *also* **litchee** /lee-chee *or* lie chee/ [Southeast Asian] a round, walnut-sized, somewhat sweet fruit indigenous to China and now widely cultivated. Fresh lychees have a fibrous hull and black central seeds, normally removed in prepared dishes. **lychee nut** dried lychee fruit.

M

ma'amoul [Middle Eastern] date-filled semolina cookies shaped in a wooden mold. *also* **ma'amul, maamoul**

maast-o-khiar *see* **mast-o-khiar**

machi *or* **macchi** /mah'-chee/ *also* **machli** /mah'-chlee/ [Indian] fish.

Madras /mah-drahss'/ [Indian] British term that implies an item is served in a hotter spicy curry sauce. Named after a city in south India, but not known by that name there.

maduros /mah-doo'-rose/ [Latin American] plantains that have been allowed to ripen fully to a sweet, fruity state and then are cut lengthwise or diagonally and fried.

maeuntang, maewoon tang /may-oon-tang/ [Korean] very spicy soup.

mafe /mah-fay/ [West African] Senegalese peanut butter stew, with mutton, chicken, or beef, cooked with various vegetables and fat. *also* **maffe, maafe**

mai fun *see* **mei fun**

makhani /mah-kah′-nee/ [Indian ("buttery")] typically, tender meat or vegetables simmered in tomato-butter curry sauce. *also* **makhni, makhan, makhanwala** /mah-kahn-wah′-lah/

maki-sushi [Japanese] sushi items rolled up in an exterior skin made of nori seaweed, typically cut into slices.

malagueta *also* **melegueta** /mah-lah-gay′-tah/ **1.** [West African, Caribbean] a hot pepper-like spice, also called Guinea pepper, made from small berries of a plant in the same family as cardamom. **2.** [Brazilian] a small hot chile pepper.

malai /mah-lye′/ [Indian] cream.

malai kofta /mah-lye′-kofe′-tuh/ [Indian] mashed boiled potatoes and cottage cheese, formed into a ball-shaped or elongated croquet, deep fried, then simmered in a creamy sauce.

malanga [Latin American] a root vegetable resembling taro, which is used in soup and stew recipes.

ma-muang /mom-wong/ [Thai] mango, not to be confused with *med ma-muang*, which is cashew nuts.

mandelbrot /monn-dul-brote/ [Jewish] sweet, twice-baked almond bread resembling biscotti.

mandu [Korean] popular dumplings made of noodle envelopes filled with ground meat and chopped vegetables, which are then fried, steamed, or made into soup. *also* **man doo, mandoo** *see also* **pot stickers**

manduguk [Korean] soup with mandu dumplings. *also* **mandoo gook**

mango chutney *see* **chutney**

mango lassi /lah′-see/ [Indian] popular sweet beverage made from yogurt, mangoes, and sugar, blended to the consistency of a light milkshake.

mango sticky rice *see* **sticky rice**

manicotti /mah-nih-cot′-tee/ [Italian] large pasta tubes stuffed with a filling and baked.

manioc /man-yock/ *see* **cassava**

manis [Indonesian] sweet.

manouri /mah-noo′-ree/ [Greek] an ancient creamy, unsalted white cheese made from goat's or sheep's milk and whey.

manti /man-tee/ [Turkish] miniature ravioli-like packets of pasta with spiced meat filling.

mantu [Chinese] plain steamed buns.

mantu [Afghan] appetizer or entree consisting of steamed dumplings filled with minced meat, chopped scallions, and other vegetables, topped with yogurt sauce.

manzo [Italian] beef.

ma po tofu [Chinese] spicy Szechuan-style dish of diced tofu in a ground pork and hot chile pepper sauce. *also* **ma-pu, ma por**

marinara /mar-ih-nar′-uh *or anglicized* mare-uh-nare-uh/ [Italian ("from the sea")] tomato-based pasta sauce with garlic and parsley.

marinate [various] to soak a food item in an acidic sauce or liquid for an extended period of time, to flavor and tenderize it. *noun* **marinade** (*Note: for safety, foods marinated for more than an hour should be kept under refrigeration.*)

Marmite® [U.K., other (from French, "stock pot")] an extremely salty, strong-flavored yeast extract spread, a by-product of beer brewing process, commonly spread on toast.

Marsala [Italian (named after a city)] a dark, sweet Sicilian dessert wine.

Marzipan /mar′-tsip-pan/ [various European] a dense almond paste commonly molded into edible miniature fake fruits and other sculpted objects, painted in realistic colors with edible coatings. May be made fresh for cake decorations (using raw egg) or prepared as a packaged product with fully-cooked ingredients.
(*Note: freshly made marzipan is made with raw egg. Foods prepared with raw [i.e., uncooked or unpasteurized] eggs may be unsafe for pregnant women, young children, older adults, and those with compromised immune systems.*)

masa /mah′-sah/ [Mexican, Latin American ("dough")] a perishable dough made from corn kernels that have been freshly boiled with lime (calcium hydroxide) and ground into meal, used to make fresh tortillas, tamales, and similar foods.

masa harina / mah′-sah ah-ree′-nah/ [Mexican, Latin American ("dough flour")] corn kernels that have been boiled with lime (calcium hydroxide), dried, and ground into a flour for storage, to be later reconstituted and used to make tortillas, tamales, and similar foods.

masala /mah-sah'-lah/ [Indian] **1.** any spice mixture. **2.** a loosely-applied term for a relatively dry curry dish prepared with a spicy, somewhat viscous gravy or sauce.

masala dosa /mah-sah'-lah-doe-sah/ [Indian] a large fried pancake made from fermented rice flour and special lentils, typically stuffed with seasoned mashed potatoes plus various other special ingredients like peas or nuts. A popular Southern Indian dish. *see* **dosa**

Masaman *see* **Massaman**

mascarpone /mah-scar-po'-nay/ [Italian] a rich, sweet cream cheese.

masoor dal *also* **masur dal** [Indian] red lentils.

Massaman curry /mahss'-sah-mahn/ [Thai] mild, sweet red curry of Muslim origin, commonly including beef, potatoes, roasted peanuts, coconut milk, cardamom, garlic, tamarind, sugar, herbs, and spices. *also* **Masaman, Mussaman, Mat saman**

mast-o-khiar [Persian] cucumber, yogurt, and mint as a side dish or appetizer. *also* **must-o-khiar, maast-o-khiar, maust khiar,** *other spellings*

masu [Nepalese] meat.

matar /muh-tar/ [Indian] green peas. *also* **mattar, mutter**

matar paneer /muh-tar-pah-neer/ [Indian] popular combination of curried peas with cubes of pressed cottage cheese.

matbucha salad [Middle Eastern] a tomato and bell pepper salsa or salad, served as a cold appetizer.

matzo /mott'-suh/ [Jewish] traditional unleavened bread-flour cracker consumed during Passover. *also* **matzoh, matzah**

matzo meal [Jewish] ground matzo (crumbs).

matzo ball soup [Jewish] traditional soup made with chicken, vegetables and one or more substantial round balls of matzo meal and shortening.

maust khiar *see* **mast-o-khiar**

med ma-muang /met-mah-mwong/ [Thai] cashew nuts, typically in a stir-fry with meat, vegetables, and chiles. *also* **met ma muang**

mee goreng /mee-go-rheng'/ [Malaysian, Indonesian] spicy stir-fried egg noodles with bean sprouts, cabbage, and seafood or tofu. *see also* **bahmi goreng**

mee krob /mee-graub/ [Thai] crispy stir-fried noodles, typically with shrimp, chicken, or pork topping and sweet-and-sour sauce.

meethi /mee'-tee/ [Indian] sweet.

mei fun, mai fun /may-foon/ [Chinese] thin rice noodles similar to vermicelli. *also* **mei foon**

mein /main/ [Chinese] thin wheat noodles.

melegueta *see* **malagueta**

melitzanes, melizanes /may-lee-dzah-ness/ [Greek] eggplant.

melitzanosalata /may-lee-dza'-no-sah-lah'-tah/ [Greek] roasted eggplant salad.

melokiyah *see* **molokhia**

menudo /meh-noo'-doe/ **1.** [Mexican] authentic hearty tripe soup or stew made from beef stomach and, typically, calf's foot, hominy, chiles, and other ingredients, cooked for several hours. A traditional holiday specialty served at any time

of day, also considered a hangover remedy. **2.**
[Filipino] a stew made with pork, tomato sauce,
and vegetables, and sometimes liver, sausage,
or chicken, typically served with rice.

merck *see* **muk**

merguez [North African] a spiced sausage made
with ground lamb, beef, fat, and natural casings.

meshoui /mesh-wee/ [Moroccan] roasted leg of
lamb with vegetables.

mesclun [various] a variable mixture of small,
young leaves from field greens, for salad.

mesir /mess'-r/ [Ethiopian] lentils, either the
whole (brown) or split (pinkish-orange) type.
also **misir, misr**

mesir alecha /mess'-r-ah-letch'-uh/ [Ethiopian]
mildly spiced lentil stew.

mesir wat /mess'-r-watt/ [Ethiopian] popular lentil stew flavored with onions and berbere (hot
pepper seasoning), served hot. *also* **misr wot**
see also **kae mesir wat**

mesob /meh-sub/ [Ethiopian] a small, decorated
table resembling a woven wicker basket, designed to hold food trays during meals.

methi /met-ee/ [Indian] **1.** fenugreek, which may
be consumed as cooked leafy greens or used as
a dried herb with a slightly bitter taste. **2.**
fenugreek seed, used to impart a unique flavor
to pickled items.

meuntang *see* **maeuntang**

mezze /may-zay'*or* mehz-uh/ [Middle East,
Greek, Turkish] **1.** a setting of very numerous
small appetizers, typically consumed with alcoholic beverages, sometimes as a meal in itself.
2. an individual small appetizer. *also* **meza,
meze**

mien /myen/ [Vietnamese] bean thread. *see also* **cellophane noodles**

migas [Tex-Mex] a mixture of eggs, tortilla chips, and many other ingredients, served for breakfast or other meals.

Milo® [Malaysian] brand name for a fortified cocoa beverage popular in southern and tropical countries.

minced [various] finely chopped.

minchet abish /min-cheh-tah-bish/ [Ethiopian] finely chopped lean beef sauteed with chopped garlic and onions, and berbere (hot pepper seasoning) or milder seasonings.

minestrone [Italian ("big soup")] a rich soup containing beans, pasta, vegetables, and seasonings.

Ming shrimp [Chinese] wok-fried shrimp with spicy hot sauce.

miondo /me-yon'-doe/ [West African] an oversized noodle similar to pasta, made from bland fermented cassava, commonly steamed and served with roasted fish or other foods.

mirepoix /meerh-(uh)-pwah/ [French] finely-diced mixed vegetables, such as onions, carrots, and celery, stewed in butter, wine, and herbs, sometimes with veal, ham, and bacon fat, used for braising or to season soups and stews.

mirin [Japanese] sweet rice wine for cooking.

misir *see* **mesir**

miso /mee-so/ [Japanese] thick brown fermented paste made of soybeans and grains, used as a flavoring in soups and sauces.

misr *see* **mesir**

misti, misto [Italian] **1.** antipasti. **2.** mixed.

mitmita /m't-m't-tah/ [Ethiopian] extremely hot pepper spice powder made from cayenne pepper, ginger, cumin, cardamom, and coarse salt.

mofongo [Puerto Rican] mashed fried plantain with pork rind, accompanied by seafood or meats.

Moglai, Moghlai *see* **Mughlai**

mohinga, mohingar [Burmese/Myanmar] spicy catfish soup or gravy served over noodles, popular for breakfast or other meals in Myanmar. Variably seasoned and garnished.

moi-moi /moy'-moy/ [West African] ground black-eyed peas in the form of a molded, steamed cake. *also* **moyin-moyin**

mojo /mo-ho/ [Cuban] a marinade or sauce featuring garlic and citrus juice.

mole /mo'-lay/ [Mexican (from Nahuatl *molle* "mixture" or "sauce")] a smooth hot sauce made of onion, garlic, tomato, chiles, and spices, and sometimes chocolate and nuts. Typically served over poultry.

molho /moh'-lyo/ [Brazilian] one of a number of mild to very hot spicy sauces used as a condiment for meats and fish.

molokhia /muh-loo'-hghee-uh/ [Egyptian, Sudanese] ancient greens soup or stew made from highly mucilaginous (i.e., gooey) chopped leaves resembling spinach or chard, typically served over rice and croutons and topped with vinegar sauce and sliced meat. *also* **mloukhia, mloukhiyeh, melokiyah, molokkhiyya, melokhia, meloukhia**

momo [Tibetan, Nepalese] steamed dumpling filled with meat, chopped vegetables, and seasonings.

mondongo [Colombian, other] tripe soup made with beef stomach, potatoes, yuca, rice, and seasonings.

Mongolian [Chinese, Mongolian] a style of cooking characterized by boiled meats, milk products, limited vegetables such as scallions, large flat ovens, and the absence of fish. Mongolia is also the birthplace of hot pot. *see also* **hot pot**

Mongolian beef [Chinese] sliced beef stir-fried with garlic, soy sauce, and scallions.

Mongolian chicken [Chinese] marinated chicken sautéed with scallions, garlic, chile peppers, and bean sauce, with soy sauce and broth.

Mongolian pork [Chinese] grilled marinated pork chops or shredded pork stir-fried with scallions and other ingredients.

moo, mu [Thai] pork.

moo goo gai pan /moo-goo-guy-pan/ [Chinese ("fresh mushrooms cooked with sliced chicken")] sliced chicken with mushrooms, stir-fried with vegetables, served in a light-colored sauce made from egg white, cornstarch, and wine. *also called* **moo goo chicken**

moo pad khing [Thai] sliced pork stir-fried with fresh ginger, onions, mushrooms, and Thai sauce.

moo shu, mu shu, moo shi [Chinese] exotic shredded vegetable mixture stir-fried with egg or slivers of marinated meat, rolled up by the diner in a thin, sturdy rice pancake with plum sauce as a condiment.

moqueca /moe-kay'-kah/ [Brazilian] a variable seafood stew typically made with coconut milk, dendé oil, and variably spicy pepper seasoning.

morcilla /more-see′-ya/ [Spanish] dark, salty sausage filled with pork blood, rice, onions, and paprika.

moros y christianos [Cuban (from Spanish, "Moors and Christians")] black beans and rice flavored with onions, garlic, and sometimes ham.

mortadella [Italian] the original Bologna sausage, a predecessor of "baloney."
(*Note: government food safety experts advise heating all deli meats or luncheon meats to steaming hot before they are eaten by pregnant women, young children, older adults, or those with compromised immune systems.*)

moussaka /moo-sah-kah′, mou-sah′-kah/ [Greek] a kind of casserole similar to shepherd's pie, with minced lamb (or beef) and eggplant in alternating layers, onions, tomato, and seasoning, topped with a white sauce (béchamel) and baked. *also* **mousaka**

moussakhan *see* **musakhan**

moyin-moyin *see* **moi-moi**

mu /mooo/ [Thai] pork.

muek, mueg *see* **muk**

Mughlai /moo-glye/ [North Indian] a rich, Persian-influenced style of cooking developed during the reign of wealthy North Indian royalty, characterized by an emphasis on wheat breads, meats, and a sophisticated balance of (usually) milder spices including cardamom, butter, cream and yogurt sauces, eggs, almonds, cashews, and rose water. *also* **Moghlai, Muglai, Moglai, Mughal**

muhalabiyyah /moo-hahl-ah-bee-ah/ [Middle Eastern] smooth semolina pudding made with milk and sugar, served cold.

mujaddarah /moo-jah′-dah-rah′/ [Middle Eastern] lentil and rice stew with sautéed onions.

muk /muhk/ [Thai] squid (calamari). *also* **mueg, muek**

muk tod /muhk-tawd/ [Thai] deep-fried squid served with Thai chile sauce.

mulligatawny soup /moo-lag-uh-twah′-nee/ [South Indian ("pepper water")] **1.** traditional spicy meat and lentil based soup with rice, lemon, and coconut milk. **2.** a variable recipe for spicy soup adapted to include numerous non-traditional ingredients, including meat or vegetarian versions.

murgh /merg/ [Indian, other] chicken. *also* **murg, murga**

musakhan /moo-sah-khan/ [Middle Eastern] chicken marinated with sumac and spices, baked on bread.

mu shu *see* **moo shu**

Mussaman *see* **Massaman**

must-o-khiar *see* **mast-o-khiar**

mutter /muh-tar′/ [Indian] green peas. *see also* **matar**

N

naan, nan /nahn/ [Indian/Pakistani, other (from Persian *noon* "bread")] flatbread, most commonly referring to **tandoori naan,** a fresh flatbread made with refined white flour, leavened and stretched like pizza dough, then baked rapidly on the hot interior surface of a tandoor (clay oven).

nabeyaki udon [Japanese] cooked wheat noodles served in piping hot broth in a ceramic vessel, topped with vegetables and seafood or gluten.

nachos [Tex-Mex] tortilla chips topped with salsa, lettuce, olives, and melted grated cheddar cheese. May include meats.

naengmyon /nung-myun/ [Korean ("cold noodles")] cold buckwheat noodles, either served with cold beef broth and garnishes or with chile sauce. *also* **naeng myun, neng myun**

nam *also* **nahm** /nomm (rhymes with "Mom")/ [Thai] water, broth, sauce, or juice.

nam man hoi /nah-monn-hoy/ [Thai] oyster sauce. *also* **namman hoi, nam mun hoi, nammon hoi**

namool, na mool [Korean] collection of assorted thin-stranded vegetables and greens, served cool, popular in hot weather.

nam pik pow *see* **prik pow sauce**

nam pla /nomm-blaah/ [Thai] salted fermented fish sauce. *see also* **nuoc mam, patis**

nam prik, nam phrik /nomm-prig/ [Thai] hot chile pepper and fermented fish sauce.

nam prik pow *see* **prik pow sauce**

nam sod /nam sought (nam rhymes with ham)/ [Thai] **1.** a traditional salad of ground steamed pork meat and pork skin prepared with lime juice, onion, peanuts, ginger, and hot chiles. Commonly consumed with beer. *also* **nam sod moo 2.** Americanized versions of nam sod made with chicken or other non-traditional ingredients.

nan *see* **naan**

nan-e barbari /non'-ee-bar-bar'-ee/ [Persian] a large round or oblong leavened-wheat flatbread made with a little bit of cornmeal, rising to about the thickness of a person's hand. Usually cut into four-inch pieces. *also* **barbari bread**

nariyal, narial [Indian] coconut.

nasi /nah-see/ [Indonesian, Malaysian] rice.

nasi campur /nah-see-chomm-poor/ [Indonesian ("rice mixture")] steamed rice served with a variety of side dishes, including vegetables, meats, and garnishes.

nasi goreng /nah-see-go-reng'/ [Indonesian] fried rice, typically mixed with shrimp and various meats, chopped cabbage, and other vegetables.

nasi lemak /nah-see-lem-mock'/ [Malaysian] popular meal consisting of a ball of rice (often cooked in coconut milk with cloves and pandan leaves), ikan bilis (tiny fried whole anchovies), sambal belacan (chile paste), peanuts, rojak, cucumber slices, and curry or spiced squid.

navratan korma /nahv'-rah-ten kor'-mah/ [Indian, Pakistani ("nine jewels korma")] a stew made with nine distinct vegetable ingredients or cubed lamb, cooked with nuts in cream sauce, usually served with rice or bread. *also* **navrattan, nauratan**

ndizi /en-dee'-zee/ [East African] plantains or bananas steamed in a banana leaf or corn husk, or pan-fried in ghee.

ndole /en-doh'-lay/ [West African] **1.** a common vegetable resembling spinach with a bittersweet taste. **2.** leafy greens cooked with peanut sauce, tomatoes, pepper, and other ingredients, especially popular in Cameroon. *also* **ndolle** *also called* **bitter leaf**

neau *see* **nua**

neng *see* **naengmyon**

Neptune's delight [Chinese] common restaurant nomenclature for fancy seafood dish.

Newari [Nepal] the predominant culture of the Kathmandu valley area. *also* **Newar**

Nicoise /nee-swahz/ [French] style of cooking from the city of Nice on the French Riviera. Common ingredients include black olives, anchovies, string beans, and tomatoes.

nigella /nye-jel′-ah/ [Indian, other] a spice, also called kalonji, resembling onion seeds.

nigiri-sushi /nih-ghee-ree-soo-shee/ [Japanese] molded rice balls topped with raw fish. (*Note: according to government food safety experts, pregnant women, young children, older adults, and those with compromised immune systems should avoid raw fish and seafood.*)

Nilgiri [Indian ("blue peaks")] a mountain region in southern India, where a unique fragrant tea is grown.

Nilgiri korma [Indian] a green stew made with ground cilantro and sometimes green chiles.

niter kebbeh /nit-r-kib′-beh/ [Ethiopian] clarified, dehydrated butter, which is flavored with garlic, ginger, salt, and spices. Used as a cooking oil, a dipping oil, and flavoring agent. *also* **niter kibbeh**

njera *see* **injera**

nopal /no-pahl′/ *plural* **nopales** /no-pah′-lehs/ [Mexican] prickly pear cactus "paddles" (with thorns removed), cooked in water.

nori /nor-ee/ [Japanese] sushi vegetable wrapping ingredient consisting of sweet-tasting, dark green to black edible seaweed in dried, thin form. Also may be served alongside meals.

norimaki /nor-ee-mock-ee/ [Japanese] a roll of sushi with nori on the outside, typically cut into slices. *see* **sushi**

Northern Indian style [Indian] loosely-applied term for certain regional styles of Indian cooking with a prevalence of wheat breads, milk products, meats, spinach, moderately spicy curries with an onion, garlic, ginger, and tomato base, and thickened gravies or sauces. The predominant styles are Punjabi and Mughlai, reflecting the influence of surrounding regions. *see also* **Punjabi, Mughlai, Rajasthani, Kashmiri**

Northern Italian style [Italian] regional cuisines with a prevalence of milk, butter, cheese, fruits, cornmeal, bread, and rice, and a relative absence of olive oil, pasta, and tomato sauces.

nua /nuaehh/ [Thai] beef, meat. *also* **nuea, neau, nuer**

nua gai /nuaehh guy/ [Thai] chicken meat.

nuer *see* **nua**

nuoc cham /nook-juhm/ [Vietnamese] dipping sauce made with nuoc mam and various sweet, hot, and sour ingredients.

nuoc leo [Vietnamese] soup broth or base.

nuoc mam /nook-mum/ [Vietnamese, other] amber-colored, fermented salted fish sauce with a pungent aroma, used to flavor many foods. *also* **nuoc nam** *see also* **nam pla, patis**

O

oeuf /uff/ [French] egg.

okonomi-yaki [Japanese] a popular fast food similar to an omelet or pancake, with highly variable toppings.

okra [various] a small, finger-like green vegetable with a firm, crisp exterior and a famously soft, slippery interior, used in various stews, especially gumbo.

okroshka /ah-kroshe′-kah/ [Russian] traditional cold summer soup made from finely chopped vegetables and kvas (a fermented bread-based beverage) and sometimes cooked meat, topped with a hard-boiled egg, sour cream, and fresh herbs. Typically made with cucumber, diced potato, carrot, or radish.

Olivier salad /oh-liv-yeh/ [Russian (named after a French chef)] a mixture of finely-chopped boiled vegetables and meats with a mayonnaise dressing, garnished with green herbs. Commonly includes potato, carrot, egg, pickles, onions, chicken, ham, or sausage. Typically served on major holidays and known as "winter salad." also **olivie, olivye, olivje**

onglet /ohn-glay/ [French] a tender cut of beef from a muscle that supports the diaphragm, which must be cooked rare.

oothapam *see* **uttapam**

opakapaka [Hawaiian] pink snapper (fish).

opor ayam /oh-pour-eye-ahm/ [Indonesian] pieces of chicken in a mildly spiced sauce made with coconut milk, turmeric, and nuts, originating from Java.

orange beef [Chinese] marinated beef stir-fried with tangy spicy sauce flavored with oranges.

orange chicken [Chinese] Hunan-style dish of deep-fried chicken prepared with orange peel and spicy sauce.

orange sauce [Chinese, French] variable sauce made from cooked orange rind, used to flavor poultry and meats.

orchata *see* **horchata**

orecchiette /or-eh-kyet'-ay/ [Italian] small pasta disks resembling small ears.

orzo /or-zo/ [Italian ("barley")] rice-shaped pasta made from wheat semolina (not barley).

osso buco, osso bucco /o-so-boo'-ko/ [Italian ("hollow bone")] veal shank (foreleg) slow-cooked with wine, herbs, and vegetables.

oyster sauce 1. [Chinese] a variable brown sauce cooked with meat or vegetable dishes, made from soy sauce, wine, starch, and sometimes oysters and MSG. **2.** [Thai] a version of oyster sauce with a stronger oyster flavor, less salt and no MSG.

oxtail [various] meat and bone of the skinned tail of beef.

oxtail stew 1. [Jamaican] beef tail slow-cooked with spices, onion, tomato, and beans. **2.** [Southern/soul food] beef tail boiled for several hours, with common vegetables and mild seasonings added, cooked to a stew-like consistency.

P

pad /pod/ [Thai] **1.** stir-fried. **2.** stir-fried rice noodle mixture. *also* **phad, pud**

Padang /pah-dahng/ [Indonesian] cuisine originating in the provincial capital of West Sumatra, known for spicy dishes.

pad kana /pod-kah-nah/ [Thai] stir-fried Chinese broccoli or broccoli leaf. *see* **kana**

pad kee mao *see* **drunken noodles**

pad prik /pod-prig/ [Thai] stir fry with hot chile pepper seasoning.

pad see-ew /pod-see-eww/ [Thai] fried broad noodles in a sweet soy sauce, usually with broccoli, egg, and a selected meat. *also* **pad see-iew, pad si-iew**

pad talay /pot-tah-lay/ [Thai] mixed seafood stir-fried with a special sauce.

pad Thai /pot tie/ [Thai] popular dish of stir-fried rice noodles, usually topped with bean sprouts, scallions, shrimp or tofu or meat, chopped peanuts, and small pieces of egg.

paella /pie-yay-ah *or* pie-ale′-yah/ [Spanish (from Valencian "pan")] **1.** popular variable casserole made with chicken, seafood, saffron rice, bell peppers, garlic and onions, and sometimes chopped sausage, traditionally cooked in a large flat pan over an open fire for more than one person. **2.** a large metal or fired clay pan used to cook paella. **3.** a faithful approximation of the original Valencian paella casserole, which was made with chicken, rabbit, pearled rice, lima beans, green beans, tomatoes, paprika, saffron, and olive oil, and without onions, sausage, or other modern amendments. *also* **Valencian paella**

pak /pock/ [Thai] vegetables. *also* **phak, puk**

pakawra, pakaura /pah-cow-rah/ [Afghan] *similar to* **pakora**

pakora *also* **pakoda** /pah-ko'-rhah/ [Indian] pieces of vegetable, chicken, or fish dipped in a spiced chickpea-flour batter and deep fried.

palak /pah-lock'/ [Indian] spinach.

palau /pah-lao/ [Afghan, other] rice dish, pilaf. *also* **pilau, polo**

palm oil [African] reddish oil popular in West African and other tropical recipes. *see also* **dendé**

Panang curry /pah-nahng'/ [Thai (named after Penang, Malaysia, near Thailand)] a type of red curry that is slightly sweeter and milder, with dishes incorporating coconut milk or peanuts. *also* **Penang curry**

pancetta /pahn-cheh'-tah/ [Italian] unsmoked bacon, which has been assembled into a roll, dry-cured, and sliced. May be fatty or very lean.

panch phoron /paunch'-for-ahn/ [Indian ("five spices")] popular Bengali mixture of whole spices, typically cumin, fennel, fenugreek, mustard, and kalonji, used with vegetables. *also* **panch phoran**

pancit, pansit /pahn-seeht'/ [Filipino] variable fried noodle dish with vegetables and meats.

pandan leaf [various] the leaf of the screwpine tree indigenous to Southeast Asia and the Pacific, used as a flavoring.

paneer, panir /pah-near'/ [Indian] freshly made cottage cheese curds pressed into a block, usually cut into cubes.

panggang *also* **pangang** /pong-gong/ [Indonesian] barbecued or roasted meat.

pangsit /pong-sit/ [Indonesian] noodle rolls or envelopes filled with ground meat paste, fried and consumed as finger food or cooked in soups. *similar to* **wonton**

pani puri /pah'-nee-poo'-ree/ [Indian] bite-sized, deep-fried circular puffed wheat breads filled with potatoes, lentils, and special spiced tamarind-flavored water, offered as a popular snack by street food vendors and restaurants. *also* **pani poori**

pansit *see* **pancit**

panzanetta /pahn-zah-neh'-tah/ [Italian] a salad made with dried bread pieces and lots of vegetables, marinated in its dressing before serving.

papa [Latin American] potato.

papa a la huancaina /pah-pah-ah-lah-wahn-kah-ee-nah/ [Peruvian] popular recipe for potatoes served with spicy cheese sauce and an egg, typically as an appetizer. *also* **papas a la huancaina**

papadum /poppa-dom/ [Indian] a very thin, brittle, spiced lentil cracker about the size of a plate. Can be deep fried, flame roasted, or even microwaved. *also* **papad, papadam, poppadom**

paper chicken [Chinese] chicken wings or morsels wrapped in paper or foil and deep fried.

papri chat /pop'-ree-chott'/ [Indian] a tangy cold snack of fried wheat crisps mixed with diced potatoes and chickpeas, topped with yogurt and a sweet, spicy tamarind chutney. *also* **aloo papri chat**

paratha /pah-rah′-tah/ *also* **parantha** [Indian/Pakistani] **1.** soft, flaky, multilayered unleavened whole-wheat flatbread, lightly pan-fried or cooked in a tandoor and splashed with butter or vegetable oil. **2.** a similar whole-wheat flatbread filled with potato, prepared lentils, or spiced ground meat.

parihuela [Peruvian] seafood served with yuca and rice.

Parma [Italian] an unusually fine version of prosciutto ham. *see* **prosciutto,** *safety note*

Parmigiana /par-muh-jhahn′/ [Italian] indicates foods such as veal or sliced eggplant, which are breaded and fried, then covered with tomato sauce and grated cheese.

parilla, a la parilla /pah-ree′-yah/ [various] on the grill.

parrillada, parillada /pah-rhee-yah′-dah/ [South Amercian] a variety of charcoal-grilled meats, organ meats and sausages on a platter.

pasanda [Indian] extremely tender strips of pounded meat or chicken, cooked in a mild, rich almond-based sauce.

pashka *see* **paskha**

paska [Ukrainian] sweet butter and egg bread with a circular shape and fancy sculpted decorations on top, traditional for Easter. *similar to* **challah**

paskha, pashka /pahs′-ka/ [Russian] a sweet cheesecake in the shape of an upside-down flower pot or truncated pyramid, typically incorporating chopped fruits and nuts. An Easter specialty, sometimes made with raw egg.

(*Note: foods prepared with raw [i.e., uncooked*

or unpasteurized] eggs may be unsafe for pregnant women, young children, older adults, and those with compromised immune systems.)

pasta e fagioli /pasta fah-jhol′-ee *or* pasta fah-zool′/ [Italian] pasta and beans in a soup with vegetables and herbs.

pasteles /pah-stay′-lace/ [Caribbean] **1.** popular dumplings made from meat and starch-bearing vegetables, wrapped and boiled in banana leaves. **2.** [South American] various sweet pastries. **3.** [Spanish] a sweet or savory pastry.

pastel tres leches /pah-stell′-tress-ley′-chase/ [Latin American] popular chilled dessert cake soaked in three kinds of milk, originally from Nicaragua. *see also* **tres leches**

pastilla *see* **bastilla**

pastirma [Turkish, Armenian] spiced slices of dried beef. *also* **basturma**
(Note: foods prepared with uncooked meat may be unsafe for pregnant women, young children, older adults, and those with compromised immune systems.)

pastitsio /pah-steet′-chee-oh/ [Greek] a kind of lasagne, usually with alternating layers of pasta and tomato-meat sauce, topped with a white sauce (béchamel) and baked. May be made with lamb or Greek cheese.

pastrami [Italian, other (derived from Turkish *pastirma*)] beef that has been preserved with salt, then smoked.

patacon /pah-tah-cone′/ [Latin American] slices of cooked green plantains, squashed flat into discs, then fried or baked with salt or other ingredients.

131

pâté /pah-tay/ [French] a popular rich meat paste traditionally made with ground meat or poultry, pork fat and herbs, slowly cooked, and served cold as an appetizer, commonly spread on bread. *also spelled* **paté, pate**
(Note: according to the government food safety experts, pregnant women, young children, older adults, and those with compromised immune systems are advised not to eat refrigerated [i.e., fresh] pates or meat spreads. Canned or shelf-stable pates and meat spreads may be eaten.)

pâté de foie gras /pah-tay-duh-fwah-grah/ [French] a special pâté made from the enlarged livers of force-fed geese, sometimes combined with truffles.

pathia, patia [Persian, Indian] **1.** a traditional fish curry made with tamarind and date sugar, a specialty of the Parsi ethnic-religious group. **2.** a variable sweet-and-sour curry dish incorporating non-traditional ingredients.

patis /pah-teece'/ [Filipino] a salted fermented fish sauce, used as a condiment. *see also* **nam pla, nuoc mam**

patrani machi [Indian] fish topped with a green chutney paste and wrapped in banana (or similar) leaf or foil, then baked or grilled, a specialty of the Parsi ethnic-religious group.

pattie [Jamaican] a curried meat and vegetable turnover. *also called* **Jamaican pattie**

peanut stew [African] *see* **groundnut stew**

peas [Jamaican, Caribbean] black-eyed peas or other beans or lentils, but not green peas.

ped /bet, pet/ [Thai] **1.** duck, as in ped-yang, pronounced "bet." *also* **pet, phed, bhet 2.** hot, spicy curry as in gaeng ped, pronounced "pet."

see **phet**

pedas /puh-doss′ *informally* puh-dis/ [Indonesian] hot and spicy. *also* **pedis, pedes**

ped-yang /bet-yaang/ [Thai] barbecued duck. *also* **phed-yang, ped-yaang** *see also* **kang-ped bhet-yang**

Peking chicken [Chinese] variable recipe of marinated chicken prepared with scallions and wrapped like a tortilla or cooked in a fancy manner.

Peking duck [Chinese] traditional fancy roasted duck, which the diner prepares by rolling up carved slices of duck breast in a thin pancake along with scallions and hoisin sauce, thus forming a small "package," which can be easily grasped and eaten. In classic versions, the skin and flesh are separated during preparation and individually seasoned and are sometimes consumed separately.

Peking shrimp [Chinese] thickly battered and deep-fried shrimp served with scallions or other vegetables.

Peking style [Chinese] general term for a style of cooking with a prevalence of wheat noodles (rather than rice), steamed dumplings, foods wrapped in pancakes, plum sauce, garlic, and scallions, and subtle variations from dishes prepared in other regions.

pelmeni /pel-may′-nee/ [Russian] popular dish of small filled dumplings similar to ravioli, usually boiled and served with sour cream or butter and traditionally consumed with shots of vodka. The common Siberian version is filled with beef, pork, or both and is served with sour cream and sometimes vinegar for dipping. Sometimes served in a clay pot.

pemmican [Native American] pulverized beef jerky blended with dried fruit and solidified animal fat, molded into cakes or bars, which are relatively non-perishable, traditionally used as trail food. *see also* **jerky**

penne /pen-nay/ [Italian] straight tubular noodles cut at an angle, with a ridged or smooth surface. *also* **penne pasta**

peperoni /peh-peh-roh′-nee/ [Italian] typically, red and yellow bell peppers.

pepperoncini /peh-puh-ron-chee′-nee/ [Italian, other] small, relatively mild light green chile peppers, either fresh or dried. *also* peperoncini

pepperoni sausage [U.S.] a spicy beef and pork sausage sliced thin and placed on top of pizza.

pepper steak [Chinese] beef steak cut into narrow strips and cooked with bell peppers, onions, garlic, and other ingredients.

peri-peri, piri-piri, pili-pili [African, Portuguese] **1.** a hot and sour sauce made of hot chile peppers, garlic, onions, tomatoes, horseradish, and lemon juice or vinegar. **2.** foods prepared with peri-peri **3.** hot chile peppers.

pescado /pes-kah′-doe/ [Spanish, other] fish.

pescado Veracruzana [Mexican] famous preparation of fish sautéed with garlic, onions, tomatoes, capers, citrus, spices, and sometimes olives. *also called* **fish Veracruz**

Peshwari naan /peh-shah-vree-non/ [Indian, named after Peshawar, Pakistan, near Afghan border] leavened flatbread stuffed with a mixture of dried fruits or nuts. *also* **Peshawari naan**

pesto [Italian ("mashed")] a variable, strong-flavored herb paste condiment, most commonly made from basil, garlic, Parmesan cheese, pine nuts, and oil.

pet /bet, pet/ [Thai] **1.** duck, as in pet-yang, pronounced "bet." *see* **ped 2.** hot, spicy curry as in gaeng pet, pronounced "pet." *see* **phet**

Pfeffernüsse /fef´-er-neese/ [German, ("pepper nuts")] small, sweet cookies spiced with cinnamon and typically nutmeg, ginger, pepper, and cloves. Traditional Christmas cookies. *also* **Pfeffernuesse**

phad *see* **pad**

phak /pock/ [Thai] vegetables. *also* **pak**

phall /fahl/ [Indian-derived] extremely hot curry made with a strong dose of hot chile peppers, developed by restauranteurs in the U.K.

phed /bet/ [Thai] **1.** hot, spicy curry, as in gaeng phed. *see* **phet. 2.** duck, as in phed-yang. *see* **ped**

phet /pet/ [Thai] hot, spicy curry. *also* **pet, ped, phed** *see also* **kaeng phet**

pho /fuh?/ [Vietnamese] popular noodle soup meal made with rice noodles and thin rare meat strips in an elaborately seasoned, piping-hot beef broth, served in large bowls, with garnishes, bean sprouts, fresh herbs, and fresh green hot chiles on the side. Consumed for breakfast, lunch, or dinner. **pho bo** /fuh? bahw/ beef pho. **pho ga** /fuh? gaah/ chicken pho.

phoenix dragon *see* **dragon phoenix**

phrik *see* **prik**

piadina /pya-dee´-nah/ [Italian] pan-fried bread made from flour and shortening. *plural* **piadine** *or colloquial* **pié** /pyeh/

pibimbap *see* **bibim bap**

picadillo /pea-kah-dee'-yo/ [Tex-Mex, other] ground beef or other meat in a spicy tomato-based sauce.

picante [Spanish, other] spicy.

pickled [various] preserved by soaking in vinegar or other specialized liquid.

pico de gallo /pea'-coe-duh-guy'-oh/ [Mexican, Tex-Mex (Spanish, "rooster's beak")] specially processed or flavored salsa.

pide /pee-deh/ [Turkish] a flatbread with a variety of meat or other topping ingredients, resembling focaccia or pizza. Sometimes molded into a canoe shape and filled with toppings.

pierogies /peer-oh'-gheez (hard g)/ [Polish, other] a small pasta dumpling filled with potatoes, cheese, seasoning, onions, or other ingredients, boiled or fried. Served hot as a main dish or side dish. *see also* **pyrohy, varenyky**

pigeon pie *see* **bastilla**

pik pow *see* **prik pow sauce**

pilaf, pilau, pilav /pee-loff'/ [Turkish, other] a salad or casserole of steamed rice or bulgur, with vegetables, oil, meats, or other ingredients added. *see* **palau, polo**

pili-pili *see* **peri-peri**

pinakbet /pea-nock'-bet/ [Filipino] ampalaya (bitter gourd) okra, string beans, tomatoes, and bagoong (strong shrimp paste) simmered with fish or pork, a favorite dish from the Ilocos region in northwest Luzon. *also* **pakbet**

pincho /peen'-cho/ [Latin American, Spanish] a small wooden skewer.

pineapple chicken [Chinese] marinated chicken, battered and fried, and cooked in a pine-apple-flavored sweet-and-sour sauce.

pineapple shrimp [Chinese] battered and fried shrimp, vegetables, and pineapple sections, in a pineapple-juice sauce.

pipián /pea-pea-yon'/ [Guatemalan, Mexican] greenish sauce made with pumpkin seeds, commonly served over chicken.

pîrâgi /peer-ogg/ [Latvian] traditional bacon buns consisting of baked rolls with chopped onions and bacon inside, usually served on holidays and festive occasions, served hot or cold. *also* **piragi**

piri-piri *see* **peri-peri**

piroshki, pirozhki /pih-rush'-kee/ [Russian] half-circle shaped pastry turnovers filled with ground meat, vegetables, fish, or eggs, baked or deep fried. Made with a yeast-leavened dough and classically about four inches in length.

pisang goreng /pea-song'-go-rheng'/ [Indonesian] fried bananas, a dessert, side dish, or snack.

pista /pea'-stah/ [Indian] pistachio.

pistou /pea-stoo/ [French] fresh basil puree made with garlic and oil, variation of **pesto**. *see also* **soupe au pistou**

pita bread [Greek, Middle Eastern, other] a simple whole-wheat or white leavened flatbread, often formed with a hollow pocket inside that can be filled with other foods.

pla /blaah/ [Thai] fish. *also* **plah, bla**

placali /plah-kah-lee/ [Cote d'Ivoire] small dough balls made from cassava roots, which have been grated, fermented, mashed, strained, and boiled.

placki /plot-zki/ [Polish] *see* **potato pancakes**

pla dook, pla duk /blaah-dook/ [Thai] catfish.

pla lard prik /blaah rod prig/ [Thai] deep-fried whole fish with hot chile sauce. *also* **pla lad prik**

pla muk /blaah-muhg/ [Thai] squid. *also* **pla muek, pla mueg**

plantain [various] tropical vegetable resembling a large banana having a starchy flesh that is cooked before eating.

pla too [Thai] mackerel.

plov [Cental Asia] sticky rice mixed with bits of lamb. *see also* **polo, palau**

plum sauce [Chinese] traditional sweet, thick condiment made from plums, bell peppers, sugar, vinegar, ginger, and spices.

po /booh/ [Thai] crab. *also* **pu, poo, bu**

po' boy [New Orleans] a sandwich made from a crusty elongated French bread roll, with a meat, seafood, or other filling.

poblano chile [Mexican, other] relatively large, dark green to brown chile pepper, considered mild to slightly hot.

poi /poy/ [Hawaiian] traditional starchy staple, made from taro root that is boiled, mashed, and fermented.

poireau /pwah-rho/ [French] leek.

pois /pwah/ [French] peas.

polenta [Italian] **1.** boiled corn meal porridge, which can be served soft or cooled to a hardened state and sliced. **2.** a dish prepared with polenta.

pollo /poy'-oh/ [Spanish] chicken.

pollo en pina /poy'-oh-en-pea'-nyah/ [Guatemalan] chicken with pineapple.

polo [Persian] rice cooked with other ingredients.

similar to **palau** *also* **polow, pulau, pollou**

pomelo *see* **pummelo**

pommes de terre /pum-duh-tair/ [French] potatoes.

pommes frites /pum-freet/ [French] french fries.

pomodoro [Italian] tomato.

pone [Southern] spoonfuls of cornbread dough deep-fried in oil.

pongal [Indian] **1.** harvest festival in Tamil Nadu state in southern India. **2.** traditional ceremonial preparation of boiled rice and lentils with palm sugar and spices, garnished with cashews.

poori *see* **puri**

popia /poh-pee´-yah/ [Malaysian] light spring roll filled with a variety of different vegetables, most often jicama, carrots, and/or yam.

porcini /por-chee´-nee/ [Italian] a large, unusually flavorful forest mushroom.

porridge [Jamaican] a variable recipe for moist ground wheat, cornmeal, or vegetable mush, commonly consumed for breakfast.

posole, pozole /po-so´-lay/ [Mexican] a hearty soup or stew made with hominy, pork, pork parts, chiles, tomatoes, garlic, onion, and vegetables.

potage /po-tajh/ [French] thicker version of a soup.

potato pancakes [German, Jewish, Polish] pancakes made from potatoes, onion, eggs, flour, and salt, popular during holidays, served with applesauce and sour cream. *see* **latkes, Kartoffelpuffer, placki, Reibekuchen**

pot-au-feu /pot-oh-fueh/ [French] **1.** a regionally-variable ancient recipe for beef and vegetables slow-cooked in a pot of water. The resulting broth is strained and often served separately, followed by the meat and vegetables, accompanied by side dishes, condiments, and bread. The usual vegetables are leeks, onions, potatoes, turnips, and carrots. **2.** modern adaptations of this recipe incorporating chicken or other non-traditional ingredients.

pot likker [Southern/Soul (var. of "pot liquor")] the flavorful broth remaining in the pot after the steaming of greens or vegetables, reputedly high in vitamins and commonly retaining a slight vinegar, shortening, or pepper flavoring.

pot stickers [Chinese] meat or vegetable-filled noodle dumplings, which are steamed, boiled, or fried.

pozole *see* **posole**

pralines /prah′-leanz, pray′-leanz/ [Cajun] variable sized candies made with pecans, sugar, cream, and vanilla.

priew /pree-ew/ [Thai] sour. *also* **preow, preaw, praw, prew**

priew wan /pree-ew-wahn/ [Thai] sweet and sour.

prig *see* **prik**

prik /prig/ [Thai] spicy, made with hot chile or pepper seasoning. *also* **prig, phrik**

prik ki nu /prig-kee-nooh/ [Thai] Thai chiles or bird's-eye chiles.

prik pow sauce /prig-pow/ [Thai] a mixture of hot red chile peppers, garlic, and onion, deep-fried and mashed with fish sauce and sugar. *also* **nam prik pow**

prik Thai /prig tie/ [Thai] white pepper. *also* **prig thai, prik tai**

primavera /pree-mah-ver′-uh/ [Italian] tomato-based pasta sauce with onion, garlic, broccoli, zucchini, and other sliced vegetables and herbs.

prosciutto /pruh-shoo′-toh/ [Italian] raw ham, salted.
(*Note: foods prepared with raw meat may be unsafe for pregnant women, young children, older adults, and those with compromised immune systems.*)

prosciutto cotto [Italian] cooked ham. *also called* **cotto**

Provencale /pro-vohn-sahl/ [French] a style of cooking from the region of southeastern France bordering the Mediterranean Sea, emphasizing the use of fresh garden vegetables (especially tomato, onion, and garlic) local common herbs, olive oil, meats, anchovies, and other seafood. *see also* **herbes de Provence, Nicoise**

provisions [Jamaican] plantains, yams, or bananas.

psomi /pso′-mee/ [Greek] bread.

pu /booh/ [Thai] crab. *see* **po**

pud *see* **pad**

puff pastry [French] English-language term for a pastry dough consisting of very numerous ultra-thin layers of wheat dough, which puffs up when baked.

puk *see* **pak**

pulau [Persian] *see* **polo**

pulgogi *see* **bulgogi**

pulpo a la Gallega /pull′-pah-ah-lah-gahl-yay′-gah/ [Spanish] baked or poached octopus with a paprika sauce, a popular festival food in Spain, served in restaurants in the U.S.

pulque /pool-kay/ [Mexican] legendary Aztec fermented beverage made from the sap of the maguey (agave) plant, nearly unavailable outside Mexico.

pulse, pulses [Indian, other] generic term for legumes, typically lentils or split peas, collectively serving as a major source of dietary protein. *see also* **dal**

pummelo *or* **pomelo** /pumm'-uh-low/ [various] an ancient citrus fruit native to Southeast Asia, with a thick yellow rind and pink, meaty flesh, considered the ancestor of the modern grapefruit and having a similar flavor. *also called* **shaddock**

Punjabi [Indian/Pakistani] Persian-influenced cooking style from the Punjab (north India and Pakistan) region, emphasizing wheat breads, milk products, lentils, chicken, and spinach and using moderately spicy curries with an onion, garlic, ginger, and tomato base.

pu pu platter *also* **po po tray** [Chinese, Hawaiian] a combination of appetizers, often designed for two or more persons, consisting of varied chicken, beef, pork, and shrimp preparations and egg rolls.

pupusa /poo-poo'-sah/ [Salvadoran] a popular flattish grilled corn-dough pie filled with meat, beans, or cheese, usually topped with pickled cabbage and eaten with a fork. *see also* **curtido**

pupusas revueltas [Salvadoran] pupusas with a combination of filling ingredients such as cheese, pork, and beans.

puri, poori /poo'-ree/ [Indian] a circular, deep-fried whole-wheat bread which puffs up like a pillow when cooked.

puttanesca /poo-tah-ness'-kuh/ [Italian ("of the prostitute")] a sauce of tomatoes, capers, black olives, garlic, anchovies, and spices with olive oil.

puto /poo-toh/ [Filipino] popular steamed cup cakes made with sticky rice flour and coconut milk.

pyrohy /peer-oh-hee/ [Ukrainian] filled dumplings, a term used interchangeably with varenyky. *see also* **pierogies**

Q

qataif *see* **kataif**

quanta /kwahn-tah/ [Ethiopian] pieces of seasoned dried beef resembling chunks of jerky. *see also* **jerky**
(*Note: foods prepared with uncooked meat may be unsafe for pregnant women, young children, older adults, and those with compromised immune systems.*)

quantee [Newar ("mixed")] a soup made with a mixture of nine different kinds of beans and bean sprouts. *also* **kwati**

quesadilla /kay-suh-dee'-yah/ [Mexican] folded flour-tortilla appetizer filled with grated cheese and salsa and other sautéed ingredients as desired.

queso /kay-so/ [Spanish, Mexican, other] cheese.

queso fresco /kay-so-fress-co/ [Mexican] a soft, crumbly fresh cheese traditionally prepared from raw cow's or goat's milk. Sometimes used with tacos, quesadillas, enchiladas, salads, and other dishes. (*Note: government food safety experts* *advise pregnant women, older adults, and those with compromised immune systems not to eat queso fresco unless it is labeled as made with pasteurized milk or is thoroughly cooked to boiling (bubbling) hot.)*

quibebe /kib-beh′-beh/ [Brazilian] spicy Bahia soup made with butternut or acorn squash.

R

rad na /rodd-nah/ [Thai] fried flat rice noodles with broccoli and gravy, usually with selected meat or tofu. *also* **lard na, lad na**

radicchio /ra-dee′-kee-oh/ [Italian] a type of chicory with a reddish leaf, usually a salad constituent.

raita /rye′-tuh/ [Indian] **1.** as usually served in the U.S., a liquidy, hand-beaten yogurt accompaniment blended with sliced cucumbers and cumin seeds, typically consumed as a contrast to hot spicy curries. **2.** traditionally, beaten yogurt with a wide variety of added vegetables or spices.

Rajasthani /rah-jah-stah′-nee/ [Indian] the semi-nomadic cooking style of the arid northwestern portions of India, characterized by an emphasis on milk products, pulses, curry-filled buns, some game meats, and a wide variety of sweets.

rajma /rah-jhmah/ [Indian] red kidney beans.

ramen /rah-men/ [Japanese] **1.** very popular slender fast-serve wheat noodles in bowls of broth topped with meat, vegetable, or seafood flavorings. **2.** a cup or package of instant freeze-dried ramen constituents, to which boiling water is added to make a noodle meal.

ranchero sauce /rahn-chair′-oh/ [Tex-Mex] a cooked sauce made from tomatoes, garlic, onion, chiles, oregano, salt, and pepper, used as a condiment.

ras el hanout /rahss-el-hah-noot/ [North African] a variable, customized spice mixture including allspice, black pepper, cardamom, cayenne pepper or chile peppers, caraway, cinnamon, cloves, coriander, cumin, ginger, mace, nutmeg, turmeric, and sometimes fragrant herbs. *also* **ras al hanout**

rasmalai, ras malai /russ-muh-lye′/ [Indian] flattened balls of spongy cottage cheese curds, boiled in syrup and served in flavored evaporated milk.

ratatouille /rha-tah-tooey/ [French] a vegetable stew made with eggplant, tomatoes, bell peppers, and zucchini, seasoned with garlic and herbs.

rava /rah′-vah/ [Indian] semolina.

recaito [Puerto Rican] mild green seasoning mixture made from peppers, cilantro, and garlic.

red curry [Thai] a dish prepared with a popular aromatic blend of hot spices and herbs, featuring dried red chile peppers and typically incorporating coriander, garlic, shallots, lemongrass, galangal, cumin, lime, salt, shrimp paste, and other ingredients. *also called* **gaeng ped, kaeng daeng, kaeng phet**

red red [West African] black-eyed peas and plantains cooked with palm oil and seasonings, originally a boarding school specialty in Ghana.

refried beans [Tex-Mex, Mexican] mashed boiled pinto beans, traditionally re-cooked in a frying pan with lard, chopped onions, and salt and variously flavored.

refritos /ruh-free-toes/ [Tex-Mex, Mexican] *see* **refried beans**

Reibekuchen [German] *see* **potato pancakes**

relleno, rellenos /ray-yay'-noce/ [Mexican] stuffed.

remoulade /rhem-oo-lodd/ [French, other] a tangy mayonnaise-mustard and herb sauce, sometimes made with raw egg.
(*Note: foods prepared with raw [i.e., uncooked or unpasteurized] eggs may be unsafe for pregnant women, young children, older adults, and those with compromised immune systems.*)

rendang /ren-dong/ [Indonesian, Malaysian] spicy beef stew prepared with coconut milk, galangal, and lemongrass.

repollo /rep-poy'-oh/ [various] Spanish word for cabbage.

res /race/ [Latin American] beef.

reshmi kebab [Indian ("silky" kebab)] delicately seasoned, marinated ground chicken morsels, or pieces of tender breast meat, skewered and broiled in a tandoor (clay oven).

reshteh /resh-tay/ [Persian] noodles. *see also* **aash-e reshteh**

revueltos [Spanish, other] mixed or scrambled.

ricotta /ree-goh'-tuh *anglicized* ruh-cot'-uh/ [Italian] a soft, sweet granulated fresh cheese made from whey, resembling small-curd cottage cheese.

rigani /ree-hyah-nee/ [Greek] oregano.

rigatoni [Italian] large grooved pasta tubes cut to short lengths.

rijsttafel /ritz′-tah-ful/ [Dutch-Indonesian ("rice table")] colonial-era meal of rice accompanied by dozens of different entrees and side dishes, now popular in South Africa and the Netherlands (but not Indonesia).

risi e bisi /ree′-zee-bee′-zee/ [Italian (from a movie)] flavored rice and peas, cooked in broth.

risotto /ree-zo′-toh/ [Italian] preparation of boiled rice mixed with other ingredients, to which broth is gradually added to produce a creamy texture.

rizogalo /ree-zo′-gah-lo/ [Greek] rice pudding sprinkled with powdered cinnamon.

rodizio /ro-dee′-zyo/ [Brazilian] a presentation of sequential courses of different grilled meats cut from the skewer at tableside.

roe [various] fish eggs.

rogan josh /roe′-gahn-joosh′, rhymes with "push"/ [Indian] a highly aromatic, spicy mutton or goat stew originally from Punjab and Kashmir, slow-cooked with dried red peppers, yogurt, and (commonly) tomatoes, with particular seasonings localized in certain regions.

rojak /ro-jack/ [Malaysian] a variable salad-like dish consisting of jicama, pineapple, green beans, cucumber, and spicy peanut sauce.

ropa vieja /ro′-pah-vyay′-hah/ [Cuban, Venezuelan (from Spanish "old clothes")] a popular stew of shredded beef and a tomato-based sauce.

Roquefort /rhok-forh/ [French (named after the village of Roquefort-sur-Soulzon)] a famous blue cheese, made from sheep's milk.
(*Note: government food safety experts advise pregnant women, older adults, and those with compromised immune systems not to eat blue-*

veined cheeses such as Roquefort unless they are labeled as made with pasteurized milk.)

roselle [African, other] hibiscus flowers used to make a naturally sweet, tart beverage. *see* **bissap juice, karkadeh, sorrel**

rose water [Bulgarian] strongly rose-scented water used as a flavoring.

roti /ro'-tee/ **1.** [Indian] a soft, griddle-baked whole-wheat flatbread, eaten with curry sauce or wrapped around curried meat or vegetables. Usually prepared without butter or yeast, it resembles a thick flour tortilla. **2.** [Caribbean] thin, rolled flatbread filled with curried vegetables or meat stuffing, sometimes fried.

roti canai /ro'-tee-chah'-nye/ [Malaysian] a simple flour-based bread tossed and layered with ghee and cooked on a flat griddle; often served with kari ayam (chicken curry).

Rotkraut [German] a popular side dish of stewed red cabbage.

rouille /rhoo'-yuh *or* roo'-ee/ [French ("rust")] **1.** a strong-tasting mayonnaise sauce made with olive oil and garlic, reddened with varying amounts of tomato, saffron, or paprika, traditionally served with fish soup or bouillabaisse. May contain raw egg. **2.** common variations of rouille made using chile peppers or red bell peppers.
(Note: foods prepared with raw [i.e., uncooked or unpasteurized] eggs may be unsafe for pregnant women, young children, older adults, and those with compromised immune systems.)

roux /rhoo/ [French, Cajun/Creole] a mixture of flour and butter or other fat or oil, used as a base for various sauces or gravies.

rugelach /ruh'-guh-luhkh/ [Jewish, Russian] traditional rolled-up cream-cheese-dough pastry with a sweet, cinnamon-flavored fruit and nut filling, sometimes with chocolate chips.

run down, run dung [Jamaican] fish or seafood stew with vegetables, hot peppers, and coconut milk, cooked down to a custard.

S

saag, sag /sahg/ [Indian] cooked greens, commonly spinach, but sometimes collard greens, kale, mustard greens, or turnip greens.

saag aloo /sahg-ah-loo/ [Indian] curried, simmered chopped greens (commonly spinach) with potato cubes.

saag paneer [Indian] curried, simmered chopped greens (commonly spinach) containing diced cheese morsels.

sabsi /sob'-zee/ [Afghan] spinach.

sabzi /sob'-zee/ *also* **sabji, subzi 1.** [Persian] fresh vegetables with selected fresh herbs, such as mint, parsley, cilantro, dill, watercress, or scallions, commonly served with bread and feta cheese. **2.** [Indian] any vegetable preparation or entrée.
(Note: government food safety experts advise pregnant women, older adults, and those with compromised immune systems not to eat feta unless it is labeled as made with pasteurized milk.)

sa cha *also* **sha cha** [Chinese] a Taiwanese sauce made from a variety of ingredients including shrimp, brill fish, peanuts, onion, garlic, chile peppers, and spices.

saffron [various] an expensive, mild, fragrant spice, often used to flavor rice, imparting an orange-red color.

sag *see* **saag**

saganaki /sah-gah-nah′-kee/ [Greek] sliced cheese slab made from cow's or sheep's milk, battered and fried, topped with lemon juice. Popular snack, sometimes splashed with brandy and ignited.

sake /sah-keh/ [Japanese] traditional rice wine served cool or slightly warmed.

salsa /sahl′-sah/ [Mexican, other] a mixture of coarsely or finely chopped tomatoes, onions, and chile peppers and their juices.

salteado /sahl-tay-ah′-doh/ [Latin American] sautéed or stir-fried. *also* **salteada, saltado**

salteñas /sahl-ten′-yahs/ [Bolivian] a baked pie-dough envelope, with a laced or pinched seam on top, filled with meat, potatoes, peas, olives, egg, spices, and other ingredients. Commonly served as a main dish. *similar to* **empanadas**

saltibarsciai [Lithuanian] cold beet soup with (sour) cream and hard-boiled eggs, flavored with dill, preferred in summer months.

saltimbocca /salt-im-bo′-kah/ [Italian, ("jumps in the mouth")] a variable recipe for preparing pounded meats with thinly-sliced ham and sage, typically in a wine and butter gravy. *also* **saltimboca, saltimbucco**

Salzburger nockerln /salts-burger-knocker-lin/ [Austrian] a fancy baked meringue dessert preparation made of mounds of whipped eggs, sugar, and sweet flavoring.

sambal /sahm-ball'/ [Indonesian, Malaysian] **1.** prepared hot chile peppers, as a mashed paste or pureed with other ingredients, as a condiment or added to cooked foods. **2.** variable recipe for dishes made with sambal, typically including beef, tempeh, or chopped chile peppers.

sambal belacan /sahm-ball' beh-la'-chan/ [Malaysian] a chile paste consisting of red chillies, shallots, lime, tamarind, sugar, and salt.

sambhar, sambar /sahm-burr'/ [Indian] a popular, spicy, tangy, soupy vegetable-lentil stew from southern India, flavored with curry leaves, coconut, and broiled mustard seeds. Usually accompanies dosas or idli.

sambosa /sam-boh-sah/ **sambosay** [Afghan] *also* **sambusa, sambussa** /sahm'-boo-sah/ [Ethiopian] trianglular pastry shell filled with seasoned ground beef or lentils, similar to a samosa.

samosa /sah-mo'-sah/ [Indian] popular triangular pastry-dough turnover filled with curried potatoes and peas and deep fried, consumed as an appetizer or snack.

sanbusak [Middle Eastern] pastry turnover filled with seasoned ground meat. *see* **sambosa**

sancocho /sahn-ko'-cho/ [Colombian, Venezuelan, Puerto Rican ("parboiled")] popular stew made from oxtail, rib of beef, hen, or other meats combined with plantains, cassava (yuca), squash, and herbs. Varies by locale.

sangak /sahng-gock'/ [Iranian] very large leavened whole-wheat flatbread, baked on hot pebbles and served very fresh from the oven, commonly with cheese and sabzi.

san shien [Chinese ("three things")] a dish with three major ingredients, such as chicken, shrimp, and beef, plus vegetables and sauce. *see* **triple delight**

sansho [Japanese] a ground spice from a type of prickly ash shrub, related to Szechuan pepper.

sapi /sah-pee/ [Indonesian] beef.

sapparot /sopp-bah-rode/ [Thai] pineapple. *also* **supparod, sapparod, saparod**

sashimi [Japanese] small slices of raw, very fresh salt-water fish, dipped in soy sauce and wasabi (Japanese horseradish) or placed on top of rounded rice morsels (nigiri-sushi) and consumed raw.
(*Note: according to government food safety experts, pregnant women, young children, older adults, and those with compromised immune systems should avoid raw fish and seafood.*)

satay, saté [Indonesian, Malaysian, other] little chunks of marinated meat or shrimp grilled on small bamboo skewers and served with spiced peanut sauce.

Sauerbraten /zour-brah-ten/ [German] beef long-marinated and stewed with vegetables and herbs, with a sweet-and-sour flavor.

Sauerkraut [German] white or green cabbage fermented in brine.

savory [various] **1.** *adj.* flavored with salt and spices or herbs. **2.** *n.* an aromatic culinary herb with a minty flavor.

sayadiya *or* **sayadiyeh** [Egyptian] lightly seasoned fish fillets dipped in flour and fried, then placed on a bed of rice and garnished.

scallopini /skah-lo-pee-nee/ [Italian] variable recipe for veal or other boneless meat which is pounded flat, mildly seasoned, battered, and lightly fried, and served with a sauce. *also* **scallopine**

scampi [Italian] **1.** shrimp partially split and grilled with butter and garlic. **2.** a very large prawn shrimp or small lobster.

scape [various] the flowering top of the garlic plant, harvested in the spring when the growth is tender, used in a similar manner to the garlic bulb.

schmaltz [Jewish] rendered chicken fat used in recipes or spread on matzos.

Schwarzwälder Kirschtorte /shvorts′-vel-duh-keersh′-tor-tuh/ [German] *see* **black forest cake**

scrapple [Pennsylvania Dutch, Southern] boiled pork parts combined with corn meal and seasoning.

Scotch bonnet peppers [various] one of the hottest chile peppers.

seaweed [Japanese] harvested or cultivated ocean vegetable products, which are typically processed or dried and consumed with soups, sushi, or other foods. *see also* **nori, kombu, wakame**

see-ew, see-iew *see* **pad see-ew**

seekh kebab /seek′-kah-bob/ [Indian] marinated, minced lamb or other variably-seasoned ground meat, molded into a sausage shape on a skewer, then charcoal broiled.

sega wat, siga wat /see′-gah-wutt′/ [Ethiopian] beef or lamb cut into tiny cubes and stewed with garlic, herbs, and hot spices.

seker pare /sheh′-kehr-pah′-reh/ [Turkish ("melt in your mouth")] popular dessert consisting of a small, soft cookie dipped in syrup.

sekuwa, sekwa [Nepalese] barbecued marinated meat with garlic, ginger, and spices.

semolina [various] a coarse, yellowish-white, high-protein flour made from durum wheat kernels (without the wheat germ or bran) that is used to make pasta, couscous, gnocchi, and other products.

semur /seh-moor/ [Indonesian, other] meat stewed with sweet soy sauce, cloves, ginger, bayleaf, onion, garlic, and macadamia nuts.

serrano chile /seh-rah´-no/ [Mexican] a very hot medium-small green or red chile pepper.

sesame chicken [Chinese] pieces of marinated chicken coated with batter and fried, then sprinkled with toasted sesame seeds.

sesame cold noodles [Chinese] appetizer consisting of cooked egg noodles topped with sesame oil and tahini dressing, served cold.

sesame shrimp [Chinese] sautéed marinated shrimp with sesame-flavored sauce.

sev /sevv/ [Indian] savory noodle-like strands made of lentil dough that has been pressed through a perforated metal disk and deep fried, consumed as a snack food.

seviche *see* **ceviche**

sha cha *see* **sa cha**

shaddock [various] a citrus fruit similar to a grapefruit, with a thick rind. *see* **pummelo**

shahi korma /shah´-hee-kor´-mah/ [Indian ("royal braised stew")] classic Mughlai dish of curried meat cubes, slow-cooked in a creamy yogurt-based sauce with almonds or cashews.

shallots /shuh-lots´ *or* shall´-uts/ [various] small buds of a plant similar to onions and scallions.

shami kebab /shah′-mee-kuh-bob′/ [Indian, other] patty-shaped morsels of minced lean mutton or other ground meat mixed with lentils, seasoned with curry spices, and deep fried or cooked on a griddle. They resemble small hamburgers.

shank [various] meat from the hind leg of an animal.

shanklish [Lebanese] seasoned goat cheese balls or morsels preserved in oil, sometimes served with other items as an appetizer.

shaslik *also* **shaslic** /shosh-lick/ [Indian (from Armenian "grilled")] chunks of marinated meat or shrimp with vegetables skewered and grilled. *similar to* **shish kabab**

shashlik /shosh-lick/ [Russian] variation of shaslik. *also* **shashlyk**

shaved ice [Malaysian, other] a shredded ice product resembling "snow-cones" that is used in various desserts. *see* **ice kacang**

shawarma, shwarma [Middle Eastern] a pita bread sandwich filled with slices of grilled marinated chicken or meat, with tomato, onion, and tahini or garlic-flavored dressing. With this cooking method, whole chunks of meat are stacked on a rotating vertical spit and roasted. *similar to* **gyro**

shchi /she/ [Russian] cabbage soup made with tomatoes and dill, with many versions including a variety of other ingredients. May be made with fresh cabbage or Sauerkraut.

shepherd's pie [English, Irish] a thick ground lamb or beef stew cooked with vegetables, topped with mashed potatoes and grated cheese, then baked.

shiitake, shitake /shee-tah-keh/ [Japanese, other] a medium-large dark brown mushroom, preferred in ethnic dishes for its herbal qualities and nutrients.

shirazi salad /shuh-rah′-zee/ [Persian] a traditional cucumber, tomato, and onion salad.

shirin polo [Persian] sweet rice, variously combined with almonds, orange peel, raisins, and other ingredients. A common wedding dish.

shiro /shoo′-ro/ [Ethiopian] spiced ground fava beans, sometimes mixed with split peas. *also* **shuro**

shiro wot /shoo′-ro-wutt′/ [Ethiopian] a classic spicy stew made from powdered fava beans with ground lentils, split peas, or chickpeas and hot pepper seasoning. Traditionally made without butter or other dairy products and consumed during fast days. *also* **shuro wat**

shish kebab, sheesh kebab [Near East to India (from Turkish, "skewer roast meat")] assorted chunks of marinated meat and vegetables, approximately 1-2 inches in size, placed on a skewer in an alternating order and roasted or grilled.

shoyu /shoy-oo/ [Japanese] traditional soy sauce.

shrimp paste [Thai, other] a pungent paste or sauce made from fermented shrimp and salt, used to flavor many Thai (and other) dishes.

shrimp scampi *see* **scampi**

shrimp toast [Chinese] flattened or pureed shrimp mixed with scallions and cooked egg yolk, attached to a piece of plain white toast and baked or deep fried. Served as an appetizer.

shrimp with cashew nuts [Chinese] stir-fried shrimp with cashews and mixed vegetables, most commonly prepared with hot chile peppers, Kung Pao style.

shrimp with lobster sauce [Chinese] popular Cantonese dish of stir-fried shrimp, which contains no lobster. *see* **lobster sauce**

shumai, shu-mei [Japanese] Chinese-style noodle dumplings filled with ground seasoned pork or shrimp, then steamed or deep fried. *see* **siu mai**

shuro *see* **shiro**

shwarma *see* **shawarma**

Sichuan *see* **Szechuan**

si-iew *see* **pad see-ew**

sigara borek /see-gah-rah-bueh-rehk/ [Turkish] a cigar-shaped pastry shell filled with feta cheese and other ingredients and fried, a popular Turkish appetizer.

siga wat [Ethiopian] *see* **sega wat**

silpancho [Bolivian] popular dish made of flattened beef fillets pounded with bread crumbs and fried, topped with fried eggs, potatoes, and salsa, served over rice.

Singapore [Asian] a style of cooking combining Malaysian, Chinese, and Indian ingredients and methods, in particular curry-spiced dishes.

siu mai, sui mei /shoo-my/ [Chinese] steamed dumplings filled with ground pork, a common appetizer or dim sum item.

sizzling rice [Chinese] cubes of rice that have been slightly overcooked in a pan or baked, then deep fried, drained, and promptly brought in contact with piping hot soup or other liquid ingredients, at which time the kernels crackle and explode.

skordalia /score-dah′-lya/ [Greek] pureed garlic-potato dip or spread made with vinegar, olive oil, and salt. Typically served cold with pita bread wedges as an appetizer.

snow peas [Chinese] flat, green, edible pods resembling pea pods, which are sweet and crisp when eaten whole and are usually stir-fried or steamed with other ingredients.

soba noodles [Japanese] long, thin, tan-colored buckwheat noodles similar to spaghetti, commonly served cold with a dipping sauce (*zaru soba*), or served warm in a bowl of broth topped with vegetables, meat, or seafood (*tempura soba*).

soffritto /so-free′-toh/ [Italian ("slightly-fried")] a sauté of meat ingredients and vegetables such as garlic, onion, parsley, and celery, used as a base to flavor soups or meat dishes.

sofrito /so-free′-toe/ **1.** [Spanish, Cuban, other] a sauté of aromatic vegetables, such as bell peppers, tomato, onion, garlic, and spices, fried with pork fat flavored and reddened with annatto. **2.** [Puerto Rican] a sautéed mixture of chopped bell pepper, chile peppers, onion, garlic, and cilantro, used as a base for cooking other foods.

sop /sop/ [Indonesian] a clear broth containing meat or vegetables but without coconut milk.

sopapillas, sopaipillas /so-pah-pee′-yahs/ [Tex-Mex] deep-fried wheat pastry puffs, commonly served with syrup and cinnamon.

sorrel [various] a family of plants with sour leaves, or the extract used in making certain beverages.

soto [Indonesian] soup, flavored broth.

soto ayam [Indonesian] a variable chicken soup

with turmeric, lemon grass, and sometimes bean sprouts, noodles, egg, or other ingredients.

soto kambing [Indonesian] goat meat chunks in coconut milk soup.

soto sapi [Indonesian] beef chunks in coconut milk soup.

soufflé /soo-flay′/ [French ("puffed up")] a variable egg casserole flavored with cheese or other ingredients that puffs up when baked and is served with a sauce.

soupe au pistou /soup-oh-pea-stew/ [French] a popular garden vegetable soup incorporating white beans, pasta, basil, and other herbs.

soupe de poireau /soup-duh-pwah-rho/ [French] leek soup. *also* **soupe au poireau** /soup-oh-pwah-rho/

soursop *see* **guanabana**

souse [Caribbean] a dish made with slow-cooked pork parts pickled with lemon or lime juice, onion, hot peppers, and spices.

Southern Indian style [Indian] loosely-applied term for several regional (often vegetarian) styles of cooking, with a prevalence of rice dishes, fermented rice and lentil flour products, relatively hotter spices, broth-like gravies or sauces, and the frequent use of coconut milk, tropical fruits, seafood, root vegetables, mustard seed, curry leaf, and pickled condiments.

souvlaki /soov-lah′-kee/ [Greek] chunks of marinated meat skewered and flame-broiled, served in pita bread with or without vegetables or tzatziki sauce. Known as "the hamburger of Greece."

soy sauce [Chinese, Japanese] traditionally, a sauce called *shoyu* made from soybeans, wheat, salt, and fermenting organisms. (Note: some commercial brands are manufactured from sugar, salt, and chemically-treated soybean derivatives.) *see also* **tamari**

Spaetzle /shpet'-sul/ [German] fresh-made wheat-egg noodles boiled in water, served as a side dish in lieu of potatoes or rice. *also* **Spätzle**

spanakopita /span-ah-ko'-pee-tah/ [Greek] popular filo dough pie or turnover filled with spinach, feta or other cheese, onions, and seasonings, typically formed into triangular pockets or squares.

Spanish omelet *see* **tortilla Española**

special tibs /t'bs/ [Ethiopian] common restaurant nomenclature for a customized "house special" preparation of diced meat pan-fried to a well-done state in a hot pepper seasoning, typically using special methods of preparation or ingredients, for example made with filet mignon, wine, or tomatoes, or served on a pot of charcoals.

Springerle /sh-pring'-er-luh/ [German ("little knights")] anise cookies molded into sculpted shapes, popular during the Christmas holiday season.

spring rolls [Chinese, Thai, Vietnamese] a mixture of (typically) ground pork, shrimp, chopped vegetables, bean thread, and seasonings, wrapped in very thin rice noodle sheets in a cylindrical form similar to (but narrower than) egg rolls and deep fried. *see also* **cha gio**

spumoni /spuh-mo'-nee/ [Italian] multi-flavor ice cream, shaped in a mold, containing little chunks of candied fruit.

ssam /sahm/ [Korean] a method of eating grilled

meat by wrapping a small portion in a lettuce leaf along with various vegetables, rice, and a spicy bean paste, picking it up and consuming it. Occasionally cabbage or squash leaves are used instead of lettuce.

stamp and go [Jamaican] deep-fried dough morsels flavored with salt fish and garlic.

steamed buns [Chinese] soft, sweet, round wheat buns commonly filled with bean paste or barbecued pork and cooked in steam.

steamed dumplings [Chinese] morsels of ground meats or seafood with chopped vegetables, wrapped in a noodle dough envelope and steamed. *see* **siu mai**

stew peas, stewpeas [Jamaican] meat and vegetable stew with kidney beans.

sticky rice [Thai] **1.** a dessert of cooked rice in a sweet syrup, served hot with pieces of fresh Mango. **2.** a type of dense, sticky rice popular in northern Thailand. *see* **khao niao**

stir-fried [Chinese, other] rapidly cooked in oil in a hot wok while being stirred or tossed, as is usually done with assorted loose ingredients.

Stollen /shto'-lun/ [German] traditional leavened Christmas bread in the form of sweet, crescent-shaped loaves made with fruits and nuts.

straw mushrooms [various] relatively small mushrooms grown in Fiji and Indonesia, preferred in ethnic dishes for their interesting flavor, appearance, and texture.

Stroganoff *see* **beef Stroganoff**

stromboli [Italian] a pizza dough envelope that has been filled with typical pizza toppings, folded over and sealed, and baked. *similar to* **calzone**

subgum, sub gum [Chinese] indicates a mixture of assorted chopped vegetables, typically onion, bamboo shoots, celery, mushrooms, bell peppers, water chestnuts, and other ingredients.

subzi *see* **sabzi**

sucuk /soo-juhk/ [Turkish] a spicy sausage made with beef and lamb.

sui mei *see* **siu mai**

sukiyaki [Japanese] a special preparation or platter consisting of very thinly-sliced beef, fresh vegetables, and grilled tofu, which are cooked at the table on a hot plate in a sweetened wine-soy sauce and which may be dipped into raw beaten egg and eaten.
(*Note: foods prepared with raw [i.e., uncooked or unpasteurized] egg may be unsafe for pregnant women, young children, older adults, and those with compromised immune systems.*)

sumac [Mediterranean] a tart spice powder ground from the dried berries of the sumac shrub. *also* **sumak**

summer rolls *see* **goi cuon**

supparod *see* **sapparot**

sushi [Japanese] **1.** a special vinegar and kelp-flavored sweetened rice. **2.** food items prepared with sushi rice, including raw ocean fish, shellfish, vegetable ingredients, and edible seaweed, usually served in an array of bite-sized morsels accompanied by dipping sauce, thin-sliced pickled ginger, and Japanese horseradish. Some examples are norimaki, nigiri-sushi, and California rolls.
(*Note: according to government food safety experts, pregnant women, young children, older adults, and those with compromised immune sys-*

tems should avoid raw fish, raw shellfish, and raw seafood.)

sweet and sour [Chinese] indicates a sauce made with sugar and vinegar, thickened with cornstarch.

sweetbreads [various] an organ meat delicacy, which is the thymus gland of a calf, lamb, or other animal.

sweetmeat [various] a small morsel of fruit or other food that is highly sweetened.

Szechuan, Sichuan /setch-wahn/ [Chinese] a style of cooking associated with the mountainous, landlocked Sichuan province in west-central China, characterized by vernacular dishes seasoned liberally with hot chile peppers and other spices, salty and pungent flavors, the use of stir-frying, garlic, pickled foods, and a variety of meats, game, and freshwater fish.

Szechuan pepper [Chinese] an indigenous sharp-flavored spice historically preceding hot chile peppers, used in Szechuan cooking and throughout China, said to have a numbing effect. Derived from berries of the prickly ash tree, it is a constituent in Chinese "five-spice" powder. *see also* **sansho**

Szechuan-style bean curd *see* **ma po tofu**

T

ta'amia /tah-mee´-uh/ [Egyptian] deep-fried balls of seasoned minced fava bean or chick pea paste. *similar to* **falafel**

tabbouleh *see* **tabouli**

tabil [Tunisian] a widely-used spice mixture made from dried hot chile peppers, garlic, caraway, and coriander.

tabouli /tuh-boo′-lee/ [Middle Eastern] a popular grain salad (pilaf) made with bulgur (parboiled wheat), chopped tomato, garlic, scallions, parsley, lemon juice, and olive oil. *also* **tabbouleh**

taco /tah-ko/ **1.** [Tex-Mex] cooked ground meat or refried beans, typically topped with chopped lettuce, grated cheddar cheese, salsa, and other condiments, served in a folded crisp-fried corn tortilla shell and eaten by hand (with some inevitable spillage of the contents). **2.** [Mexican] cooked meat, seafood, or vegetable ingredients rolled up by the diner in a soft corn tortilla.

tacos al pastor /tah′-koze-al-pah-store′/ [Mexican] tacos made with carved chunks of specially roasted marinated pork, flavored with pineapple and reddened with annatto, traditionally cooked in the form of a stack of meat assembled on a vertical spit.

tadka *see* **tarka**

tagine, tajine /tah-jheen/ [Moroccan] **1.** a spicy slow-cooked stew of meat, fish, or chicken with vegetables, dried fruits, and seasonings, usually served with bread. **2.** a round, traditionally clay (or cast iron) cooking vessel with a special cone-shaped lid for making tagines. **3.** a serving dish with a conical lid. **4.** [Tunisian] a variable stew of chopped meats or fish, vegetables, beans, and flavorings, mixed with eggs and cheese and baked in an earthenware vessel to form a crusty quiche-like casserole.

tagliatelle /tah′-glee-uh-tell′-eh/ [Italian] relatively wide ribbon-shaped noodles.

tahini /tuh-hee′-nee/ [Middle Eastern] pure sesame paste with a natural oily component.

tahu [Indonesian] tofu.

tajine *see* **tagine**

takrai /tah-cry/ [Thai] lemongrass.

talay [Thai] mixed seafood.

tamal /tah-mahl′/ **tamales** /tah-mahl′-ess/ [Mexican, other] thick cornmeal dough flavored with chopped meat or other ingredients, wrapped in a corn husk and slow-cooked with steam.

tamari /tuh-mar′-ee/ [Japanese] an aged, fermented soy sauce with a strong flavor and a substantial salt content, traditionally wheat-free.

tamarind /tam′-uh-rend/ [various (from Arabic "Indian date")] the sour, fragrant, reddish-brown, fruity pulp collected from pods of the African tamarind tree, now grown widely in India and the tropics, commonly used for making sauces or juice.

tandoor /tahn-doorh′/ [Indian] ancient-style clay pit oven with charcoal burning at the bottom, used for grilling meats and for baking bread on the hot clay sidewalls.

tandoori /tahn-doo′-rhee/ [Indian/Pakistani] cooked tandoori style, meaning baked or broiled in a tandoor (clay oven). Tandoori-style meats are generally marinated and seasoned thoroughly before cooking.

tandoori chicken /tahn-doo′-rhee/ [Indian] chicken marinated in yogurt and spices and broiled in a tandoor, typically a half bird or whole bird at a time, usually having a reddish hue imparted by a dye.

tandoori naan /tahn-doo′-rhee-non/ [Indian] a fresh flatbread made with refined white flour, leavened and stretched like pizza dough, then baked rapidly on the hot interior surface of a tandoor (clay oven).

tapas /tah′-pahss/ [Spanish] a series of small appetizers, traditionally served with alcoholic beverages, sometimes extended into a meal. *singular* **tapa**

tapenade /tah-pen-nod/ [French] a paste made from black olives, olive oil, garlic, anchovies, and sometimes capers, used as a condiment, spread, or dip, from the region of Provence.

tapioca [various] the dried granules of a starch derived from the cassava root, used as a thickening agent in pudding.

taquitos /tah-kee′-tos/ [Mexican] small rolled-up tortillas filled with meat or chicken and deep fried, commonly offered as finger food.

tarama /tah-rah-mah′/ [Greek] carp roe caviar.

taramosalata /tah-rah-mo-sah-lah′-tah/ [Greek] a dip made from mashed red caviar whipped with olive oil, typically served with crackers or pita as an appetizer. *also* **taramasalata**

tarator 1. [Bulgarian, Madedonian] traditional soup or salad made with cucumber, garlic, and yogurt, served cold. **2.** [Middle Eastern] a dip made with tahini, garlic, and lemon but no chickpeas. **3.** [Turkish] a puree of nuts, tahini, garlic, and lemon juice, as a sauce or dip.

tarka *or* **tadka** /tah(d)r-kah/ [Indian] a seasoning method, called tempering, of placing spices (along with garlic, ginger, onion, etc.) in hot oil or butter, then adding them to other ingredients at the end of the cooking process.

tarka dal [Indian] spicy simmered lentil curry with tarka-style seasoning.

tarkari /tahr-kah-ree/ [Nepalese, other] generic term for a vegetable curry in spicy broth.

taro [Asian origin, widespread use] a tropical plant having a starchy root, which is boiled and pounded into a paste (known as poi), and edible leaves, which are used to make a kind of calaloo.

tartufo /tar-too′-fo/ [Italian] truffle.

tavuk /tah-vook/ [Turkish] chicken.

t'bs *see* tibs

tchigae *see* **chigae**

tea sauce [Chinese] a sauce made with tea leaves.

teff, tef /teff/ [Ethiopian] an unusually nutritious cereal grain native to Ethiopia, used to make injera, the essential sponge bread of Ethiopia. It is a variety of millet with naturally-occurring yeast and therefore requires no additive for leavening.

tej *also* **t'ej** /tedge/ [Ethiopian] a potent wine made from honey and flavored with an indigenous variety of hops.

telur, telor /teh-loor/ [Indonesian] egg.

tempeh /tem′-pay/ [Indonesian] a flavorful, high-protein product made with fermented soybeans formed into a dense cake, sometimes also containing grains.

tempura [Japanese, other] vegetables, fish, or shrimp coated with batter and deep fried, served with a dipping sauce. *also* **tenpura**

tenderloin [various] a tender boneless cut of meat taken from the lower-middle back portion of a butchered animal.

teriyaki [Japanese] *adj.* made with teriyaki sauce.

teriyaki sauce [Japanese] a combination of soy sauce, wine, sugar, and seasonings, often used as a marinade and for basting grilled items.

Tex-Mex [Southwestern U.S.] an adaptation of Mexican-style cuisine as modified and served in the U.S., with a prevalence of meat-based chili, refried beans, flour tortillas, crispy-style corn taco shells, fried entrees, yellow cheese, and thick sour cream, and with less emphasis on soups, fresh tacos and salsas, whole beans, and white cheese.

Thai chiles [Thai] small, thin red or green chile peppers described as searing hot. *similar to* **prik ki nu, bird's eye chiles**

Thai coffee [Thai] thick, dark-roast coffee served in a glass of ice with sweetened condensed milk in the top half.

thalay *see* **talay**

thali [Indian] **1.** a combination platter with a diverse collection of food items, usually served on a metal tray with concave indentations or multiple smaller bowls. For example, a typical vegetarian thali may include lentil, rice, vegetable and yogurt preparations, bread, salad, chutney, papadam, and pickles. **2.** a metal tray or platter used to serve a thali.

thiebou dieun /cheb'-oo-jen'/ [Senegalese] rice cooked with tomato sauce, served with fish and vegetables. *also* **tiébou diene, cheb-oo-jen, chebjen, ceebu jën,** other spellings

thiebou yapp /cheb'-oo-yopp'/ [Senegalese] rice with stewed meat and vegetable sauce.

thit /teeht/ [Vietnamese] meat.

thod *see* **tod**

thukpa /took-pah/ [Tibetan] Himalayan stew with

noodles, various meats or vegetables, and spices.

tiakri /cha-kry/ [Senegalese, other] a sweetened couscous and cream dessert. *also* **thiackry, thiakry, caakiri**

tibs /t'bs/ [Ethiopian] indicates a meat or fish item sautéed or pan-fried to a well-done state, rather than rare or raw. *also* **t'ibs, t'bs**

tibs wat /t'bs wutt/ [Ethiopian] pan-fried cubes or chunks of prime beef simmered with berbere (hot pepper seasoning).

tikka /tih'-kah/ [Indian] small pieces of boneless chicken, fish, meat, or vegetables, usually marinated and grilled kabab style.

tikka masala *see* **chicken tikka masala**

timatim salad /tim-uh-tim/ [Ethiopian ("tomato")] a salad of fresh tomatoes, onions, green peppers, and squeezed lemon juice. Sometimes includes cold boiled potatoes or carrots.

tiramisu /teer-ah-me'-soo/ [Italian ("pick-me-up")] a popular exquisite dessert assembled from lady fingers, mascarpone (cream cheese), chocolate, espresso, raw eggs, and liquor.
(*Note: foods prepared with raw [i.e., uncooked or unpasteurized] eggs may be unsafe for pregnant women, young children, older adults, and those with compromised immune systems.*)

ti're /teh-(d)ray'/ [Ethiopian] raw meat (such as kitfo or sega) served warm with butter and hot spices. (*Note: foods prepared with raw meat may be unsafe for pregnant women, young children, older adults, and those with compromised immune systems.*)

tiropita /tee-ro'-pee-ta/ [Greek] a buttery, triangular filo dough pastry stuffed with cheese, as an appetizer. *also* **tyropita**

tobiko [Japanese] usually reddish egg mass from a flying fish.

tod, thod /tawd/ [Thai] deep-fried or pan-fried.

tod mun /tawd-munn/ [Thai] deep-fried morsels of spicy mashed fish or shrimp, sometimes served with a dipping sauce or cucumber relish. *also* **tod man**

tod mun khao pod [Thai] corn fritters, commonly served with a pickled condiment.

toenjang *see* **doenjang**

tofu, tou fu [Chinese] a soft, moist soybean curd product typically served cut into cubes as protein to augment vegetable dishes. It is neutral-tasting but easily absorbs other flavors and seasonings. Sometimes ground into a salad. *also called* **bean curd**

tom /tawm/ [Thai ("to boil")] indicates hot soup.

tom kha gai /tawm-kah-guy/ [Thai] popular, spicy chicken and coconut-milk soup made with galangal, lemongrass, and mushroom.

tom yum [Thai] /tawm-yum/ popular, spicy lemongrass soup with galangal in a clear broth, usually including shrimp, sliced chicken, or other meat. *also* **tom yam**

torshi [Persian] pickled vegetables.

Torte /tor´-tuh, *anglicized* tort/ [German, from Austria] generic term for any decorated rich cake with a filling or frosting of cream, fruit preserves, and nuts.

tortellini /tor-teh-lee´-nee/ [Italian] small stuffed pasta packets twisted into a crescent-shaped ring.

tortellone /tor-teh-lo´-nee/ [Italian] large pasta sheet wrapped around a filling and twisted into a crescent-shaped ring.

tortilla /tor-tee′-ya/ [Mexican] **1.** a thin, disk-shaped patty formed from corn kernels that have been boiled with lime (calcium hydroxide) and ground into meal. **2.** a soft tortilla made from wheat flour and shortening, called a flour tortilla.

tortilla Española /eh-span-yo′-lah/ [various] a beaten egg preparation made with potatoes and onions, carefully fried on both sides and served hot or cold. *also called* **Spanish omelet**

tostada /toe-stah′-dah/ [Tex-Mex] a crisp-fried corn tortilla piled with beans, meat, shredded lettuce, tomato, grated cheese, guacamole, and salsa.

tostones /toe-stone′-ess/ [Cuban, Dominican] *same as* **patacon**

tow goo [Chinese] straw mushrooms.

tres leches /tress-ley′-chase/ [Latin American] a sweet dessert made with three kinds of milk, for example cream, condensed milk, and evaporated milk. *see also* **pastel tres leches**

triple delight [Chinese] common nomenclature for shrimp, chicken, and beef (or pork) with mixed vegetables. *see* **san shien**

truffles 1. [French, Belgian, Italian] an expensive delicacy consisting of an irregular roundish fungus that grows underground, approximately one-half inch to three inches in size, usually harvested near oak trees with the assistance of specially trained pigs or dogs. **2.** a fancy chocolate candy ball dipped in chocolate powder.

tsimmes *see* **tzimmes**

tuba /tu-bahh′/ [Filipino] the fermented juice of the coconut palm flower, used to make alcoholic beverages or a uniquely flavored vinegar.

tuna [Mexican, Southwestern] cactus fruit.

Tung Ting shrimp *see* **Lake Tung Ting shrimp**

Turkish delight [Middle Eastern] a chewy confection made with sugar, cornstarch, nuts, and rose water, typically cut into small cubes and coated with powdered sugar. *also called* **lokum**

twice-cooked, double cooked [Chinese] indicates an item cooked twice, such as baked then deep fried, so that the interior is tender and well done and the exterior is crisp.

tyropita *see* **tiropita**

tzatziki /dzah-dzee′-kee/ [Greek] cucumber and yogurt dressing with garlic and herbs.

tzimmes /tsim′-ess/ [Jewish, other] variable recipe for fruits and vegetables mixed together and cooked into a sweet concoction. Popular constituents include carrots, sweet potatoes, and raisins. *also* **tsimmes**

U

udang /oo-dong′/ [Indonesian, Malaysian] shrimp.

udon /oo-don/ [Japanese] light-colored noodles similar to linguine, made from wheat.

Udupi /oo′-doo-pea/ [Indian] a town and district on the SW coast of India, famous for a style of vegetarian cooking emphasizing coconut, dosas, cashews, mustard seed, and curry leaf.

UGLI®️ fruit /ugly *or* hoo'-glee/ [Jamaican] an almost seedless hybrid citrus fruit with reddish-orange colored flesh and an irregular rind, a cross between a grapefruit and a mandarin orange or tangerine. *also called* **uniq fruit**

umeboshi [Japanese] very salty, sun-dried, long-aged, pickled sour plums, said to have medicinal effects.

upma /oop'-mah/ [South Indian] breakfast dish of semolina simmered with seasoned lentils and vegetables. *also* **uppama**

urad dal /oo'-rahd-dahl'/ [Indian] a small, flavorful, dark-skinned variety of lentil, also known as black gram, used in dal makhani and other preparations, sometimes peeled to make white lentils and lentil dumplings.

uttappam /oo'-tah-pahm/ [South Indian] a soft pancake made with fermented rice and lentil batter, topped with vegetable ingredients.

V

vaca /vah-kah/ [Spanish, other] cow.

vaca frita /vah-kah-free'-tah/ [Cuban] shredded beef steak with carmelized onions and mojo (garlic-citrus sauce).

vada /vah-dah/ *plural* **vadas** /vah-dahs/ *or* **vadai** /vah-dye/ [Indian] deep-fried lentil flour fritters, commonly donut-shaped, usually served with sambhar and coconut chutney or a yogurt-based dressing. *see also* **dahi vada**

Valencian paella *see* **paella**

vandalu *see* **vindaloo**

varenyky *also* **vareniki** /vah-ray'-nyee-kee/

[Ukrainian] traditional half-circle shaped dumplings filled with potatoes, cheese, or meat, generally boiled and served warm with sour cream. A sweet version is filled with cherries. *similar to* **pierogies** *see also* **pyrhohy**

veau /voe/ [French] veal.

Vegemite® [Australian] a salty, strong-flavored yeast extract with caramel and malt extracts. *similar to* **Marmite**®

vegetable alecha /ah-letch′-uh/ [Ethiopian] vegetable stew, relatively mildly seasoned.

vegetable bhaji *see* **bhaji**

vegetable biryani /bihr-yah′-nee/ [Indian] a fancy rice casserole flavored with saffron, various curried vegetables, and nuts.

vegetable pakora /pah-ko′-rhah/ [Indian] pieces of assorted vegetables, for example cauliflower, bell peppers, or onions, dipped in a chickpea batter and deep fried, typically as an appetizer. Resembles tempura. *see* **pakora**

vegetable samosa /sah-mo′-sah/ [Indian] deep-fried turnover filled with spiced potatoes and sometimes peas and other ingredients.

Veracruzana *see* **pescado Veracruzana**

vermicelli /verma-chelly/ [Italian] thin spaghetti.

Vichyssoise /vee′-shee-swahz/ *or* /vish′-ee-swahz/ [U.S., derived from French] a thick cream-of-leek soup with potatoes, usually served cold.

vindaloo, vandalu /vin-dah-loo′/ [Indian (from Portugese *vinha d'alhos*)] meat, fish, or vegetables (most commonly chicken or lamb) prepared with vinegar, garlic, sometimes potatoes, and tomatoes in an intensely hot spicy curry.

vinegret /vin-neh-gret/ [Russian] cooked vegetable salad featuring beets, potatoes, carrots, onions, and pickles, with dressing.

vitello /vih-tel'-lo/ [Italian] veal.

vitellone /vih-tel-loh'-nee/ [Italian] veal from a younger calf.

W

waan *see* **wan**

wafu [Japanese] **1.** a "fusion" style of preparing traditionally Western foods, such as hamburgers or fried jumbo shrimp, using Japanese methods or ingredients.

wahn, wah *see* **wan**

wakame /wah-kah-meh/ [Japanese] a type of seaweed that is dried and reconstituted in water and used in salads and soups.

wala [Newar] marinated.

wan /wahn/ [Thai] sweet. *also* **waan, wahn, wah**

wasabi /wah-sah'-bee/ [Japanese] green-colored horseradish paste (combined with mustard powder), normally provided with sushi as a substitute for the traditional grated wasabi plant harvested wild in Japan. Commonly sold in powdered form and reconstituted with water.

wat /wutt/ [Ethiopian] meat or vegetable stew made with onion, garlic, and ginger. Usually implies a spicy dish prepared with a hot red pepper seasoning, although milder versions may be found. *also* **wot, watt, we't,** *other spellings*

water chestnuts [Chinese, other] the crisp, bland, edible tuber of an aquatic plant, commonly sliced into coin-sized disks.

waterzooi [Belgian] chicken vegetable leek soup, consumed as an entree.

Welsh rarebit [U.S. and U.K., derived from Welsh] a simple preparation of melted cheddar cheese sauce poured onto toast.

we't *see* **wat**

Wiener Schnitzel /vee′-ner-shnit′-sul/ [French-German ("Viennese cutlet")] veal or beef pieces pounded flat, then breaded and fried.

winged bean [various] a tropical bean with edible pods and flowers.

wonton, won ton [Chinese] a dumpling made of small bits of pork wrapped in an oversized, floppy flat noodle, commonly served in soup or deep-fried.

won ton soup [Chinese] a popular soup made with wontons floating in a salty clear broth flavored with herbs.

woon sen [Thai] bean thread. *see also* **bean thread, cellophane noodles, glass noodles**

wor bar, wor ba [Chinese] indicates an item served over "sizzling" rice, usually in a tableside demonstration, which causes the rice kernels to crackle and explode.

wor hep har [Chinese] jumbo shrimp wrapped in bacon.

wot *see* **wat**

X

xacuti /sha-koo′-tee/ [Indian] very hot, spicy Goan-style curry made with bird's-eye chiles and coconut, for vegetarian or chicken dishes. *also* **xacutti**

Y

y-, ya- *see* **ye**

ya assa tibs /yah′-sah-t′bs/ [Ethiopian] pan-fried trout or fish. *also* **ye'assa t'bs**

yakitori [Japanese] charcoal-grilled chicken or chicken parts and vegetables on a skewer, a popular after-work meal served in specialized restaurants.

yam [African, other] a large, variable, starchy tropical tuber, very different from the U.S. yam (sweet potato).

yang /yahng/ [Thai] roasted, grilled, or barbecued. *also* **yaang**

yard-long beans *see* **long bean**

yassa /yah′-sah/ [Senegalese] chicken or fish that is marinated and simmered in lemon juice with onions, traditionally served on a platter of rice.

yat *or* **yat gaw mein** [Chinese] thick, light-colored wheat noodles commonly served in a piping hot broth or with a sauce.

yatakilt *see* **atakilt**

yataklete kilkil /yah-tuh-kuh-lay-tay-k'l-k'l/ [Ethiopian ("boiled vegetables")] name given to a vegetable stew recipe flavored with ginger and spices, not normally encountered in restaurants.

ye-, ya-, y- [Ethiopian] a common prefix added to certain words that roughly translates to "the" or "of" or "your" and does not substantially alter the meaning of the word that follows. For example, *yemisir wat* means the same as *mesir wat*.

yebeg [Ethiopian] lamb.

yeduba *see* **duba**

yellow curry [Thai] a spicy dish with an aromatic blend of spices and herbs featuring dried hot yellow chile peppers and typically including coriander, garlic, shallots, lemongrass, galangal, cumin, lime, salt, shrimp paste, and other ingredients.

yellow rice [South African] rice cooked with turmeric, cinnamon, sugar, and raisins.

yemisir wat *see* **mesir wat**

yesiga wat *see* **sega wat**

yetakelt *see* **atakilt** *see also* **yataklete kilkil**

yetimatim *see* **timatim**

yogurtlu /yo-gurt-loo/ [Turkish] made with yogurt.

yook [Korean] beef. *see also* **yuk**

Yorkshire pudding [UK, other] a hot pudding traditionally made from milk, flour, eggs, and melted animal fat.

yuca *also* **yucca** /yoo-kah/ [various] **cassava.**

yu hsiang /you-shang/ [Chinese] a sweet, hot, spicy garlic sauce. *also* **yu shiang, yu shang, yu shion** *see also* **garlic sauce**

yuk [Korean] beef. *see also* **yook**

yum [Thai] salad, mixture, mixed.

yum nua /yum-nueh/ [Thai] grilled beef salad with onions and lemon juice. *see also* **nua**

yum pla /yum blaah/ [Thai] fish salad.

yum pla muk /yum blaah-muhk/ [Thai] squid salad.

yu shiang *see* **yu hsiang**

Z

za'atar /zah-tar/ [Middle Eastern] spice mixture featuring thyme, sesame, and ground sumac, sometimes with onions and salt. *also* **zahtar, zaatar, zatar, zaater**

zabaglione /zah-bah-lyo'-neh/ [Italian] sweet cooked egg yolk custard made with Marsala or white wine. May be served warm or chilled, sometimes prepared with wild berries or whipping cream.

zafrani /zah-frah-nee'/ [Indian] made with saffron.

zahlouk [Moroccan] a cooked salad made with eggplant, tomatoes, paprika, cumin, garlic, and olive oil.

zahtar *see* **za'atar**

zakuska /zah-koose'-kah/ [Russian] an appetizer. *plural* **zakuski** /zah-koose'-kee/ cold appetizers or hors d'oeuvres, collectively, when served.

zarda palau /zar-dah-pah-lao/ [Afghan] saffron rice with sugar, orange rind, and nuts, usually served with chicken.

zarzuela /zahr-zway'-lah/ [Spanish ("operetta")] a mixed seafood stew.

zatar *see* **za'atar**

zilzil /zill-zill/ [Ethiopian] beef cut into long, thin strips, typically marinated in awaze spices and used in stew, pan-fried, or made into *quanta* (jerky).

ziti /zee-tee/ [Italian] pasta tubes, often baked in a casserole with tomatoes, cheese, seasonings, and other ingredients.

zuppa /dzoo'-pah *or* zoo'-pah/ [Italian] soup.

zuppa inglese /dzoo'-pah-in-glay'-zeh/ [Italian ("English soup")] a fancy dessert served on special occasions, made with a creamy cake custard dressed with liqueur.

Zwiebelkuchen /tsvee'-bul-koo-hghen/ [German] onion pie made with bacon, eggs, and sour cream, somewhat like a quiche or a pizza, served hot. A regional dish from the Alsace-Lorraine and Black Forest areas.

SELECTED BIBLIOGRAPHY

The wealth of printed material about ethnic foods and cooking is well known. However, a number of outstanding references are included here for their breadth and depth of information or for the quality or uniqueness of their content.

For anyone desiring more in-depth education about ethnic foods, the very best source is Eve Zibart's 427-page paperback, *The Ethnic Food Lover's Companion*, a worldwide, narrative treatment of the entire subject, reporting expansively on the history, geography, and culture of ethnic foods, including home recipes and "how to order and eat like a native." Readers interested in a dictionary with more emphasis on European, American, and Japanese foods should seek the classic *The New Food Lover's Companion* (3rd edition) by Sharon Tyler Herbst, which weighs in at 772 pages and contains alphabetical entries similar to this book and which is probably more manageable than the gigantic, expensive, and authoritative *Larousse Gastronomique*.

Alejandro, Reynaldo. *The Philippine Cookbook*. New York: Putnam, 1985. ISBN 0-399-51144-X

Algar, Alya Esen. *The Complete Book of Turkish Cookery*. London: Kegan Paul International, Ltd. 1985. ISBN 0-7103-0101-4

Batmanglij, Najmieh Khalili. *The New Food of Life: A Book of Ancient Persian and Modern Iranian Cooking and Ceremonies*. Washington: Mage Publishers, 1992. ISBN 0-934211-34-5

Bhumichitr, Vatcharin. *Vatch's Southeast Asian Cookbook*. New York: St. Martin's Press, 1997. ISBN 0-312-18274-0

Chapman, Pat. *Pat Chapman's Curry Bible*. London: Hodder and Stoughton, 1997. ISBN 0-340-68037-7

Devi, Yemuna. *The Vegetarian Table, India*. San Francisco: Chronicle Books, 2000. ISBN 0-8118-3033-0

Dewitt, Dave and Arthur J. Pais. *A World of Curries, From Bombay to Bangkok, Java to Jamaica, Exciting Cookery Featuring Fresh and Exotic Spices*. Boston: Little Brown and Company, 1994. ISBN 0-316-18224-9

Elliot, Rose. *Complete Vegetarian Cuisine*. New York: Pantheon Books, 1988. ISBN 0-394-57123-1

Galbraith, Whitney H. and Anne T. *European Menu Translator*. Reno, NV: Creative Minds Press, 2002. ISBN 0-9679591-4-4

Greer, Anne Lindsay. *Cuisine of the American Southwest*. New York: Harper and Row, Publishers, 1983. ISBN 0-06-181320-6

Hafner, Dorinda. *A Taste of Africa*. Berkeley CA: Ten Speed Press, 1993. ISBN 0-89815-660-2

_____, *Dorinda's Taste of the Caribbean*. Berkeley CA: Ten Speed Press, 1996. ISBN 0-89815-836-2

Harris, Jessica B. *Africa Cookbook, Tastes of a Continent*. New York: Simon and Schuster, 1998. ISBN 0-684-80275-9

Herbst, Sharon Tyler. *The New Food Lover's Companion, Third Edition*. Hauppauge, NY: Barrons Educational Series, Inc., 2001. ISBN 0-7641-1258-9

Jaffrey, Madhur. *Madhur Jaffrey's A Taste of the Far East*. New York: Carol Southern Books, 1993. ISBN 0-517-59548-6

Kennedy, Diana. *The Cuisines of Mexico*. New York: Harper and Row, 1986. ISBN 0-06-181481-4

Kittler, Pamela Goyan and Kathryn P. Sucher. *Cultural Foods: Traditions and Trends*. Belmont, CA: Wadsworth/Thompson Learning, 2000. ISBN 0-534-57339-8

Law, Ruth. *The Southeast Asia Cookbook*. New York: Donald I. Fine, Inc., 1990. ISBN 1-55611-214-9

Manjon, Maite. *The Gastronomy of Spain and Portugal*. New York: Prentice Hall Press, 1990. ISBN 0-13-347691-X

Merkato Market, The. *Taste of Ethiopia, the Other Good Food*. Washington: Merkato Publications International, 1991. ISBN 0-99654626-6-8

Mesfin, Daniel J. *Exotic Ethiopian Cooking*. Falls Church VA: Ethiopian Cookbook Enterprises, 1990. ISBN 0-9616345-1-0

Montaigne, Prosper, ed. *Larousse Gastronomique*. New York: Clarkson Potter, 2001. ISBN 0-609-60971-8

Moosewood Collective, The. *Sundays at Moosewood Restaurant.* New York: Simon and Shuster, 1990. ISBN 0-671-67990-2

Ortiz, Elisabeth Lambert. *The Book of Latin American Cooking*. Hopewell NJ: The Ecco Press, 1994. ISBN 0-88001-382-6

Pines, Derek A. *International Culinary Dictionary.* Chichester, UK: Summersdale Publishers, 1996. ISBN 1-873475-63-2

Sahni, Julie. *Classic Indian Cooking.* New York: William Morrow and Co., 1980. ISBN 0-688-03721-6

Shulman, Martha Rose. *The Food Lover's Atlas of the World.* Richmond Hill, Ontario: Firefly Books, 2002. ISBN 1-55297-571-1

Weiss-Armush, Anne Marie. *The Arabian Delights: Mediterranean Cuisine from Mecca to Marrakesh.* Los Angeles: Lowell House, 1994. ISBN 1-56565-126-X

Zibart, Eve. *The Ethnic Food Lover's Companion*. Birmingham AL: Menasha Ridge Press, Inc., 2001. ISBN 0-89732-372-6

SELECTED WEB REFERENCES

An excellent online food dictionary:
http//www.recipegoldmine.com/glossary/
glossary.html

Caribbean recipes:
http://www.rotishops.com/recipes.html

African recipes:
http://www.congocookbook.com

Turkish food distinctions and glossary:
http://www.sallys-place.com/food/ethnic_cusine/
turkey.htm

Restaurant links for your city:
www.zagat.com
www.digitalcity.com

100,478 recipes by Leon Brocard:
http://www.astray.com/recipes

Ray's list of Weird and Disgusting Foods:
http://www.weird-food.com
http://www.andreas.com/food.html

An archive of ethnic recipes
http://recipes.alastra.com

The Cook's Thesaurus, an online encyclopedia
with beautiful color pictures, descriptions,
synonyms, pronunciations, and suggested
substitutions:
http://www.foodsubs.com

Tyler Cowen's Ethnic Dining Guide, informative
reviews of restaurants in the greater Washington
DC area:
http://www.gmu.edu/jbc/Tyler/diningnewest.htm

A good central source of recipes, many ethnic:
http://www.recipecottage.com

The Lonely Planet Guide with detailed discus-
sions of the food and culture of each country and
region:
http://www.lonelyplanet.com/destinations

Links to worldwide recipes for ethnic foods:
http://www.recipesource.com

Over 2,000 recipes cataloged:
http://www.recipeland.com

A large online culinary dictionary covering
many ethnic food items:
http://www.epicurious.com/cooking/how_to
/food_dictionary

A site with links to many other ethnic food
glossaries:
http://www.unlv.edu/Tourism/glossary [case
sensitive]

A prodigious glossary of food facts and trivia:
http://www.foodreference.com/html/
triviatips.html

A series of unique, credit-card sized menu
translators for European travelers is available at:
http://www.TravelersMenuReader.com

Three authoritative websites regarding food
safety:
http://vm.cfsan.fda.gov/~dms/FC99guid.html
http://vm.cfsan.fda.gov/~mow/foodborn.html
http://www.cfsan.fda.gov/~dms/adlister.html

http://foodallergy.org/ is the website for the
Food Allergy and Anaphylaxis Network.

INDEX BY ETHNICITY

Colombian

Cote d'Ivoire (Ivory Coast)

Middle Eastern

Pocket Dictionary of Ethnic Foods

Thai, continued

Pocket Dictionary of Ethnic Foods

FEEDBACK AND CORRECTIONS

Readers are encouraged to submit suggestions or corrections to the text of future editions of this book. The author particularly invites suggestions to include common ethnic foods which were omitted from this book. He also welcomes different or additional definitions, different pronunciations, or different or additional assignments of nationality or ethnicity. If you would like to contact the author regarding any suggestion or improvement to the book, please refer to the contact information below. All submissions will be gratefully received.

Mailing address:
Daniel Blum
c/o Word Craft Publishing
P.O. Box 55001
Washington DC 20040-5001
Email: daniel.blum@verizon.net

Give the Gift of the

Pocket Dictionary
of Ethnic Foods

to Your Friends and Colleagues

Check your leading bookstore or order here

❏ **YES**, I want _____ copies of the *Pocket Dictionary of Ethnic Foods* at $9.95 each, plus $2.98 shipping per book (D.C. residents please add $.57 sales tax per book). Canadian orders must be accompanied by a postal money order in U.S. funds. Allow 15 days for delivery.

My check or money order for $_____ is enclosed.

Please charge my: ❏ Visa   ❏ MasterCard
                      ❏ Discover   ❏ AmEx

Name _____

Organization _____

Address _____

City/State/Zip _____

Phone _____

Email _____

Card # _____

Exp. Date_____ Signature _____

Please make your check payable and return to:

Word Craft Publishing
P.O. Box 55001
Washington, DC 20040-5001

Call your credit card order to:

1-800-480-0209

Fax: 202-291-6186